GW01280994

GOOD HOUSEKEEPING'S
New Basic Cookery

New

Compiled

GOOD HOUSEKEEPING'S
Basic Cookery

IN PICTURES

by Good Housekeeping Institute

Ebury Press London

All Rights Reserved. No part of this publication may be reproduced, stored in a retrieval system, or transmitted, in any form or by any means, electronic, mechanical, photocopying, recording or otherwise, without the prior permission of the Copyright owner.

ISBN 0 7181 3003 0

*© Copyright 1966 by
The National Magazine Co. Ltd.
Chestergate House, Vauxhall Bridge Road,
London, S.W.1.*

*Printed and bound in Yugoslavia by
Mladinska Knjiga, Ljubljana.*

*First published in this version 1966
Reprinted 1967, 1969
Revised 1970
Reprinted 1972*

Contents

PAGE		
	8	Breakfast
	20	Fish
	33	Meat and Poultry
	60	Vegetables
	66	Salads
	72	Cheese and Cheese Cookery
	80	Rice and Pasta
	84	Soups
	87	Sauces and Stuffings
	92	Pastry
	102	Batters
	107	Hot Puddings
	120	Cold Puddings
	131	Sweet Sauces
	133	Rolls, Bread, Scones
	137	Cakes and Biscuits
	164	Appendix—Cooking Equipment, Sensible Shopping, Foods in Season, Glossary of Cookery Terms, Cooking Guide and Metric Conversion Tables
	170	Index

Foreword

Real, basic commonsense cooking: that's just what we set out to explain in this new-look version of an old favourite book. We at Good Housekeeping have a unique understanding of what the brand-new cook wants to know, because so many brand-new cooks write to us with their troubles. Therefore, when we decided to re-write our best-selling Basic Cookery, to bring it absolutely up-to-date, we took the opportunity of including in it all the things we most often get asked about. Quite literally, we tell you the best way to boil an egg (we also tell you how to roast a joint and bake a cake) and we have made the instructions just as clear and simple as we know how to. But even more important than the words, are the pictures! There are hundreds of them illustrating the vital stages of the recipes and showing how the finished dish should look.

The whole book has been planned and recipes selected to make sure that even a novice can rapidly reach the stage of being able to produce a full scale —and delicious—meal; all the recipes are for 4 people.

And do remember, we are here to help you in every way we can, so don't hesitate to get in touch with us at the address below if you need advice and information.

Carol Macartney
Principal

Good Housekeeping Institute,
Chestergate House,
Vauxhall Bridge Road,
London, SW1V 1HF

Colour Plates

16	Kippers for Breakfast
17	Tomato Omelette
32	Cheesy Grilled Fish
33	Roast Sirloin of Beef
64	Salads
65	Favourite Cheeses
80	Spaghetti Bolognese
81	Stuffed Green Peppers
128	Strawberry Shortcake
129	Steamed Jam Sponge
144	Apricot Amber
145	Quick Iced Cakes

Breakfast

Below: Preparing and sugaring grapefruit

Weekday breakfasts tend to become a hurried, skimped affair of a piece of toast and a quick cup of tea—the old-fashioned hearty breakfast is now a weekend or holiday treat. However, it is important to start the day with an adequate even if light meal. Many people find cereal or fruit, followed by toast and marmalade, are quite sufficient, but some families require a more substantial breakfast with something cooked.

Any cooked dish for breakfast use needs to be quickly prepared, so frying and grilling are the most popular methods to use. To save time in the morning, it is a good plan to lay the table the night before and to leave ready everything that will be needed for the meal.

Breakfast Fruits

Almost any fresh or stewed fruit is suitable for eating at breakfast, either alone or mixed with cereals; it is usually served simply in individual dishes. If necessary, fresh fruit may be prepared overnight, though as this results in loss of the valuable vitamin C, it should not be done as a general rule. Fruit juices are another popular breakfast item; both fresh and canned juices are used, either "neat" or diluted with a little water. The most usual ones are grapefruit, orange, pineapple and tomato juices, but the juice of other fruits, such as black-currants or raspberries, may be served when in season. (To obtain the juice from soft fruit, simmer it gently with a little water until tender; strain or sieve and sweeten to taste.)

Grapefruit

Cut the fruit in half, free the flesh from all pith and membranes and remove the centre core and the pips, using a special tool or a small knife. Sprinkle with sugar if you wish.

Oranges

Peel the oranges, removing as much as possible of the white pith, then slice fairly thinly across the segments, as seen in the photograph. Flick out any pips with the point of a knife. Sprinkle with sugar if the oranges are sharp.

Swiss Apple Muesli

4 level tbsp. rolled oats
   or fine oatmeal
¼ pint fruit juice (approx.)
4 dessert apples
4 tbsps. cream or top
   of the milk
1 tbsp. honey
A little brown sugar
2 oz. sultanas or raisins
A few chopped nuts
   (walnuts, almonds, etc.)

Place the oats and fruit juice in a bowl and leave overnight. The next day grate the apples (with their skins on); keep a little back for decoration and mix the rest with the remaining ingredients (except the nuts); Put into glasses, top with some grated apple and sprinkle with chopped nuts.

Dried Fruit

Prunes and figs should be washed, then soaked for some hours (or overnight) in fresh water. Cook them in this water, adding 4-6 oz. sugar per pint; stew gently till tender and serve cold.

Top row: Swiss Apple Muesli and Prunes
Bottom row: Oranges and Dried Figs

Breakfast

Porridge and Cereals

Porridge made with Rolled Oats

1 pint water
Salt to taste
1 teacupful rolled oats (about 2 oz.)

Heat the water and when it is boiling sprinkle in the oats, stirring vigorously with a wooden spoon. Continue to stir and boil for about 5 minutes, then add salt to taste; serve very hot.

When special brands of rolled oats are used, the manufacturers directions on the packet should be carefully followed.

Prepared Cereals

There are many popular ready-to-serve cereals on the market, which require no preparation at all. They may be served with hot or cold milk and sugar or with fruit —fresh, canned or stewed. If the packet has been open for a few days, some of these cereals may be improved if they are spread out on a tin or heatproof dish and heated through in a warm oven until they regain their original crispness.

Below: Porridge and Cereal with Fruit

Sausages

Both pork and beef sausages may be used for breakfast, either grilled or fried; they are usually served with fried bread and if liked with tomatoes or mushrooms. Sausage-meat may be made into flat cakes, which are fried or baked.

Fried Sausages

Cook them gently in a little hot fat, browning them evenly. It is important to cook slowly, so that the skins do not split and so that the insides are thoroughly done. Allow about 12-20 minutes, according to size.

Grilled Sausages

Cook under a fairly hot grill, turning frequently until evenly browned and cooked through; allow about 15-20 minutes.

Kidneys

Sheep's, calf's and pig's kidneys have a better flavour and are more acceptable for breakfast dishes than ox kidney, which is more suitable for pies or stews. Kidneys served with bacon make a good substantial breakfast. Allow 1½-2 kidneys per person.
Grilling: Soak the kidneys in warm salted water, then remove the skin and cut each kidney in half. Cut out the core with sharp scissors, wash again thoroughly, thread the kidneys on to skewers, brush over with fat or oil and grill for 10 minutes.
Frying: Prepare as described above, but dip the kidneys in a little seasoned flour and fry in hot fat for 10 minutes.

Tomatoes

Cut in half, sprinkle with salt and pepper, put a knob of butter on each cut surface and grill lightly for about 5 minutes.

Fried Bread

Heat some fat in a frying pan and fry the slices of bread until crisp on both sides.

From top to bottom:
Frying and grilling
sausages; Skinning
and coring kidneys

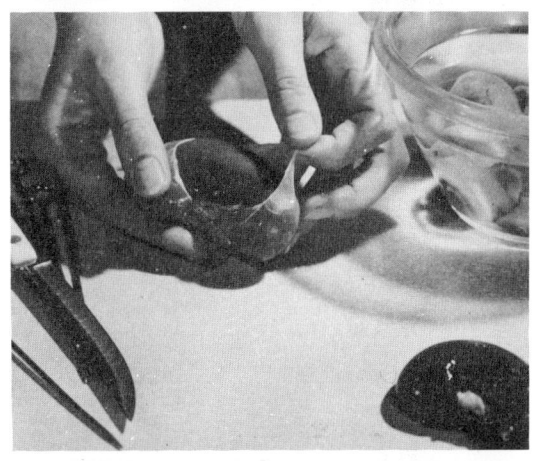

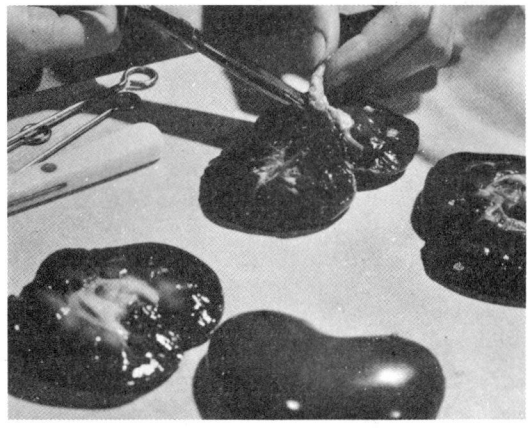

Breakfast

Bacon

Bacon, either fried or grilled, and served with a fried egg and fried bread, is probably the favourite English breakfast dish. When buying bacon remember that the fat should be firm and white and the lean a deep pink. Back, streaky, collar or gammon rashers are all suitable for both frying and grilling. Bacon is usually sliced rather thinly, but gammon is generally preferred cut a little thicker. Unless the bacon is very lean, no extra fat is needed for frying and grilling.

To prepare bacon for cooking, cut off the rind and remove any bones with kitchen scissors. To make sure that the rashers will be quite flat when cooked, snip through the fat at intervals. If on the other hand you like a wavy effect in the cooked rashers, smooth them with the flat of a knife.

Lay the bacon flat in the pan and fry it on both sides; cook it very gently, especially at first, while the fat is melting.

To grill bacon, put it under a hot grill, turning it frequently. Lean rashers must be brushed with fat before cooking.

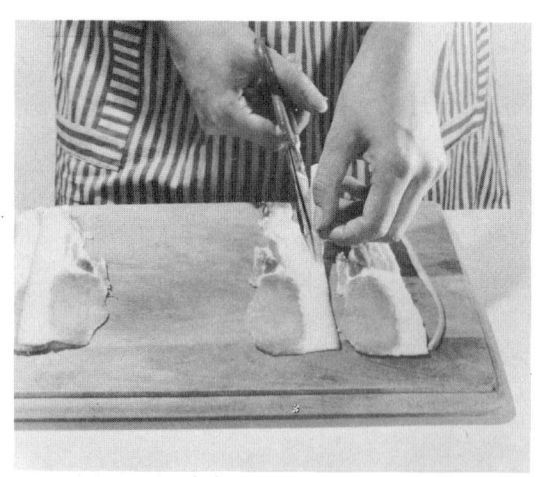

Top row: Rinding and snipping bacon;
Bottom row: Frying and grilling bacon

Fish

Smoked fish, such as kippers, bloaters and haddock, are quickly prepared and cooked for breakfast.

Kippers

Kippered herrings may be purchased boned or unboned, wrapped or unwrapped, frozen or fresh.

When serving whole kippers, allow 1-2 per person, according to size. Prepare by washing in cold water, then cutting off the heads, small fins and tail, using kitchen scissors. Put the fish into a frying pan, cover with boiling water and poach gently for about 5 minutes. Add some butter before serving (see colour picture facing page 16). Alternatively, reduce the poaching time to 2-3 minutes, then dot the kippers with butter and cook under a hot grill for 5 minutes. They can also be baked in a fairly hot oven (400°F., mark 6) for 10-15 minutes.

To reduce the rather unpleasant smell from kippers, they may be cooked in a covered dish or jug: pour on boiling water and cover closely with lid or plate. Leave for 5 minutes, pour off the water and finish cooking as liked.

Smoked (dried) Haddock

When it is intended for breakfast, smoked haddock is often served poached (i.e., simmered in a little milk, milk and water or water), but its distinctive, pleasant flavour also makes it very suitable for made-up dishes requiring cooked fish—for example, kedgeree, the recipe for which appears in the Fish chapter.

Poached Haddock

Wash the fish and cut off the tail and any fins; if the haddock is large, cut into pieces. Place in a pan, just cover with a little milk and water and cook very gently for 10 minutes. Drain and serve with a knob of butter.

Golden Fillets

Wash the fish, trim and put in a frying pan, just cover with milk and water and simmer for 8-10 minutes, or until cooked; drain and serve with a knob of butter on each fillet.

From top to bottom:
Poaching Kippers;
Grilling Kippers;
Poached Haddock

Breakfast

Eggs

Boiled

Cooking and serving; Slicing hard-boiled eggs

Breakfast cookery is easy with eggs; they can be quickly cooked in a variety of ways, as described here and overleaf, and can also be made into savoury omelettes, stuffed with bacon, fish, mushroom or other well-flavoured fillings. (See Index for omelette recipes.)

Hens' eggs are generally used for breakfast dishes, but fresh duck, turkey or goose eggs may be used if available. Turkey and goose eggs are large, so allow about 7 minutes for boiling. Duck eggs must be cooked very thoroughly, so they should not be served soft-boiled.

Boiled Eggs: Allow 1 or 2 per person and lower them gently into a pan of boiling water. For soft-boiled eggs, allow 3-4 minutes after the water has started to boil again. For hard-boiled eggs, allow 10 minutes; when they are to be used as a garnish, slice neatly or cut with a special cutter.

Poached Eggs: Simmer some water gently in the lower pan of the poacher and melt a small knob of butter in each compartment. Break the eggs one at a time and put into the compartments; season lightly, cover and simmer gently for 3-4 minutes, or until lightly set. Serve on hot buttered toast.

Baked Eggs: Heat the oven to fairly hot (400°F., mark 6). Place small pieces of butter in individual dishes and put in the oven to melt. Break the eggs one at a time and put in the dishes. Season lightly and bake just above the centre of the oven for 5-8 minutes.

Fried Eggs: Heat some lard in a frying pan. Break each egg into a cup, drop carefully into the hot fat and cook gently until set, basting with hot fat so that the eggs cook on top.

Scrambled Eggs: Melt 1 oz. butter slowly in a saucepan. Break 4 eggs one at a time into a basin, add 4 tbsp. milk and some seasoning, then beat slightly. Remove the pan from the heat, pour in the egg mixture, return the pan to the heat and cook, stirring all the time, until the mixture is creamy. Serve on hot buttered toast.

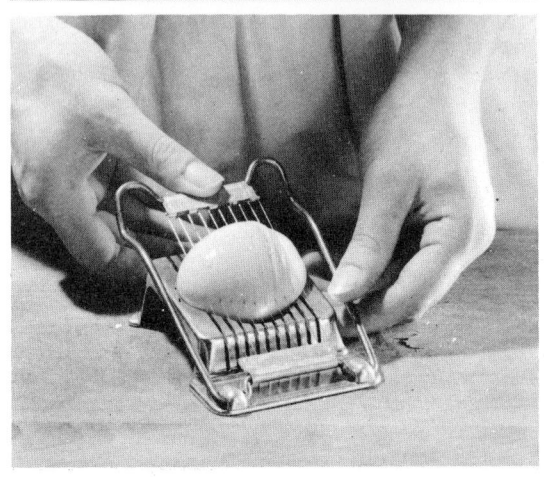

Poached

Greasing cups, cooking and serving

Baked

Preparing and serving in heat-proof glass dishes

Breakfast

Eggs

Fried
*Cooking the eggs (see p. 14)
and serving with bacon*

Scrambled
*Mixing, cooking (see p. 14)
and serving the eggs on toast*

Kippers for Breakfast: P. 13

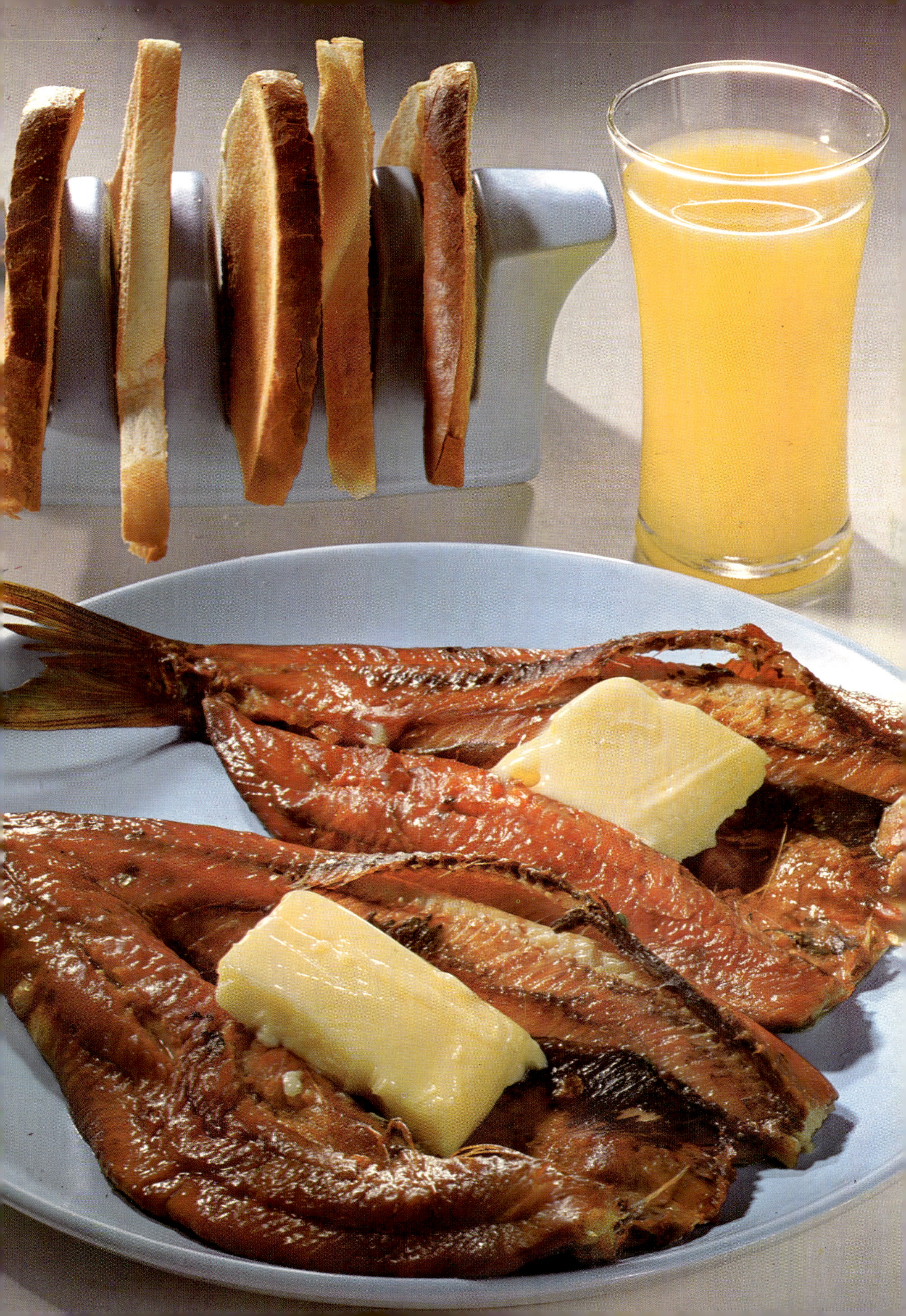

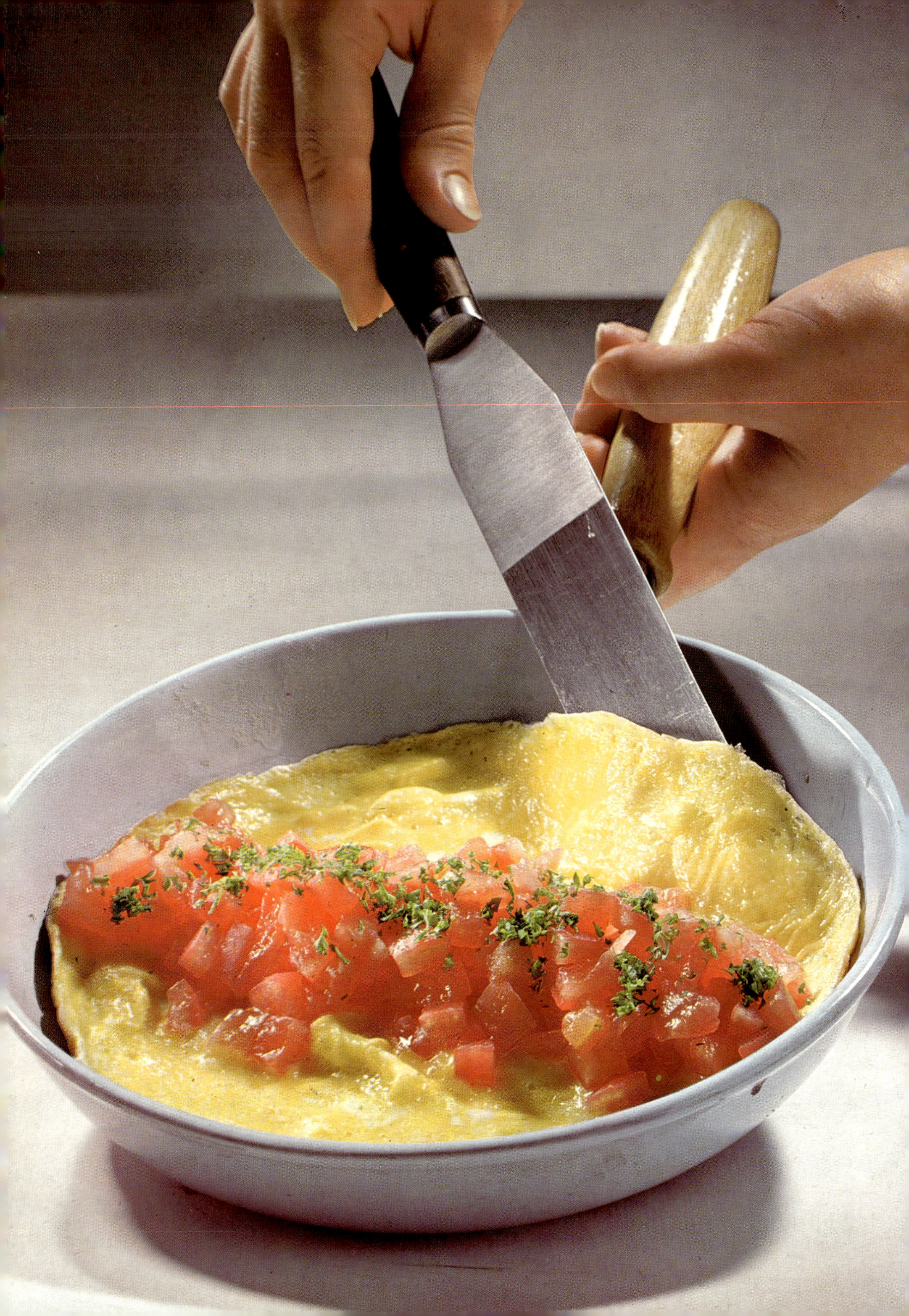

Tomato Omelette

1 oz. butter
1 tomato, skinned and chopped
Salt and pepper
2 eggs
2-4 tsps. water
Chopped parsley

Melt half the butter in a saucepan and lightly fry the tomato, adding a little seasoning. Lightly whisk together the eggs, water and some seasoning. Heat the remaining ½ oz. butter in the prepared frying pan, tilting it so that the inside surface is evenly greased. Pour in the egg mixture and gently stir the mixture towards the centre with a fork, keeping the back of the prongs flat against the base of the pan, so that the uncooked egg can flow to the sides of the pan and cook.

Once the egg has set, stop stirring and cook the omelette for another minute, until the underside is golden-brown. Put the cooked tomato down the centre of the omelette and sprinkle a little chopped parsley over it. Using a palette knife, fold one-third towards the centre, over the filling, then fold the opposite third to the centre. (See colour picture opposite.) Turn the omelette on to a warm plate, with the folded sides underneath.

The filling may be varied as you wish. Bacon, kidney, fish and mushrooms should be previously cooked; chopped ham or grated cheese may be included without further preparation.

If you prefer, serve the omelette plain, with no filling or extra flavouring.

Preparing the filling, cooking and filling the omelette and folding it ready for serving

Tomato Omelette: opposite

Breakfast

Coffee

Good coffee may be made in several ways and it is not essential to have special equipment. Whichever method is followed, however, you must use fresh coffee and sufficient of it. For a good brew, allow 2 oz. coffee (4 level tbsps.) to 1 pint of freshly boiled water; black coffee (usually served after lunch or dinner) should be made really strong and may require an even larger quantity. For breakfast it is usual to serve coffee with hot milk—generally 1 part milk to 2 parts coffee. The milk should be hot, but never boiled, and is served in a separate heated jug.

All the equipment must be kept scrupulously clean or the coffee will be unsatisfactory.

Making Coffee in an Earthenware Jug

Find out the approximate capacity of your jug so that you know the amount of water required. Warm the jug, then put in the required amount of coffee. Pour on fast-boiling water, stir vigorously, cover the jug with a saucer or folded cloth and keep in a warm place to infuse for about 10 minutes. Pour off the coffee into a warmed coffee pot (straining it through muslin or a strainer). If the coffee is not to be used at once, reheat it in a pan before serving—do not boil.

Making Coffee in a Saucepan

Put the measured quantity of coffee and water in a saucepan and place over the heat. Stir well and bring almost to boiling point, then remove the pan from the heat, stir the coffee, cover the pan and leave in a warm place or over a very low heat for about 5 minutes. Strain the coffee into a heated jug.

Making Coffee in a Percolator

Place the measured or weighed coffee in the perforated basket and put the required amount of freshly drawn water in the base of the percolator. Bring the water to the boil, then lower the heat and allow the water to percolate through the coffee for 8–10 minutes. Remove the coffee basket from the percolator and serve the coffee at once.

Making Coffee in a Cona Machine

Place 1 pint water in the lower bowl and put on to heat. Place the filter on the neck of the upper bowl and put in 2 oz. ground coffee. When the water in the lower bowl boils, fit the upper bowl on top. Allow the water to rise to the upper bowl. Draw the machine from the heat and allow the water to run back into the lower bowl. Return the Cona to the heat, so that the process is repeated once.

Filter Coffee

Place a filter paper in the filter attachment and put 1 oz. ground coffee into it. Pour 1 pint boiling water slowly over the coffee grounds, allowing it to filter through slowly until the liquid reaches the level of the spout in the lower container.

Instant Coffee

This provides a very quick, easy way of making coffee. Allow 1 level tsp. of instant coffee powder per cup. Fill the cups three-quarters full with boiling water and top up with warm or cold milk.

EARTHENWARE JUG

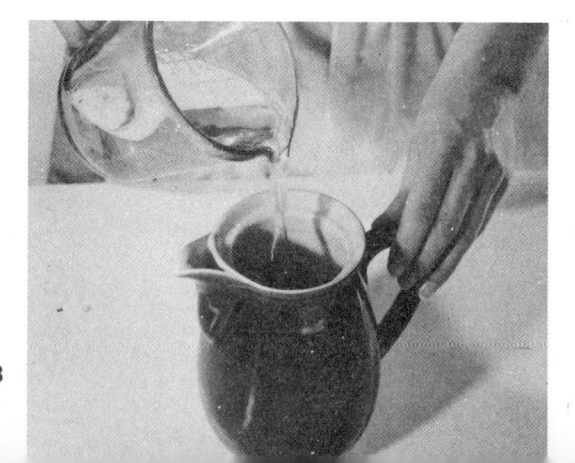

PERCOLATOR

FILTER

CONA MACHINE

Fish

Choosing Fish

1. The flesh should be firm and moist—never either watery or dried up.
2. With small whole fish like herrings and mackerel the body should be firm, with the scales still attached.
3. The eyes should be bright and not sunken.
4. Though there will be a characteristic "fishy" smell, this must not be strong and unpleasant.

Types of Fish

Cod. A large, white-fleshed fish, which can be bought as fillets, steaks and cutlets. Cod can be grilled, fried or baked or used in made-up dishes. As its taste is not strong, it needs careful seasoning and flavouring. It is usually fairly cheap.

Haddock. Another large, white-fleshed fish, with rather more flavour than cod. Haddock can be bought as fillets, steaks and cutlets and cooked by most methods.

Smoked, Dried or Finnan Haddock, that is, a fairly small haddock, split open and smoked on the bone. It has an excellent flavour and is traditionally served poached or grilled. When cooked and flaked, it can be used in made-up dishes such as Kedgeree. Golden fillets (or cutlets), as the name implies, have the backbone removed before they are smoked.

Hake. Similar to cod, but with firmer white flesh. It can be cooked by any method suitable for cod.

Halibut. A large flat fish, usually sold in slices or steaks. It has white flesh and a delicate flavour and is one of the more expensive kinds of fish. It is usually grilled, baked or poached.

Herrings. A fairly small, round-bodied fish with a silvery skin and creamy-fawn flesh, with a distinctive flavour. Herrings have a mass of small bones which make many people dislike them, but if they are correctly filleted by the fishmonger, most of the bones can be removed. Herrings are cheap and are sold whole or filleted. They are suitable for grilling, frying, baking and sousing.

Kippers. These are herrings split open and brined and smoked on the bone. Good kippers have an excellent flavour and can be poached and/or grilled.

Mackerel. A round-bodied fish, similar to a herring but usually slightly larger; it has a characteristic green and black marbling on the skin. Like the herring, it has a fawn-coloured flesh with a distinctive flavour, and it also has a lot of fine bones. It is sold whole or filleted. The flesh of mackerel is close-textured and the fish can be grilled, baked or soused.

Plaice. A flat fish with a dark grey top skin dotted with characteristic closely-set orange-red spots. The flesh is white, with a very delicate flavour. Plaice, which is quite expensive to buy, is usually sold filleted; it is cooked by grilling, frying, steaming and baking.

Salmon. A large fish with silvery skin and a deep orange-red flesh that has a firm, close texture and distinctive flavour. Salmon is a very expensive fish; it is sold in steaks and as tail end and middle cut pieces; when small, the fish are sometimes sold whole. It is suitable for poaching, grilling and baking and can be served either hot or cold.

Sole. A flat fish, more oval in shape than plaice, with a darkish brown-grey skin. It is an expensive fish and can be bought filleted or whole. Sole is cooked by grilling, frying, baking and steaming.

Turbot. A very large flat fish usually sold in thick slices or cutlets. It is a delicious and expensive fish, but its white flesh is firm in texture, so a large amount is not required. It can be poached, baked or grilled.

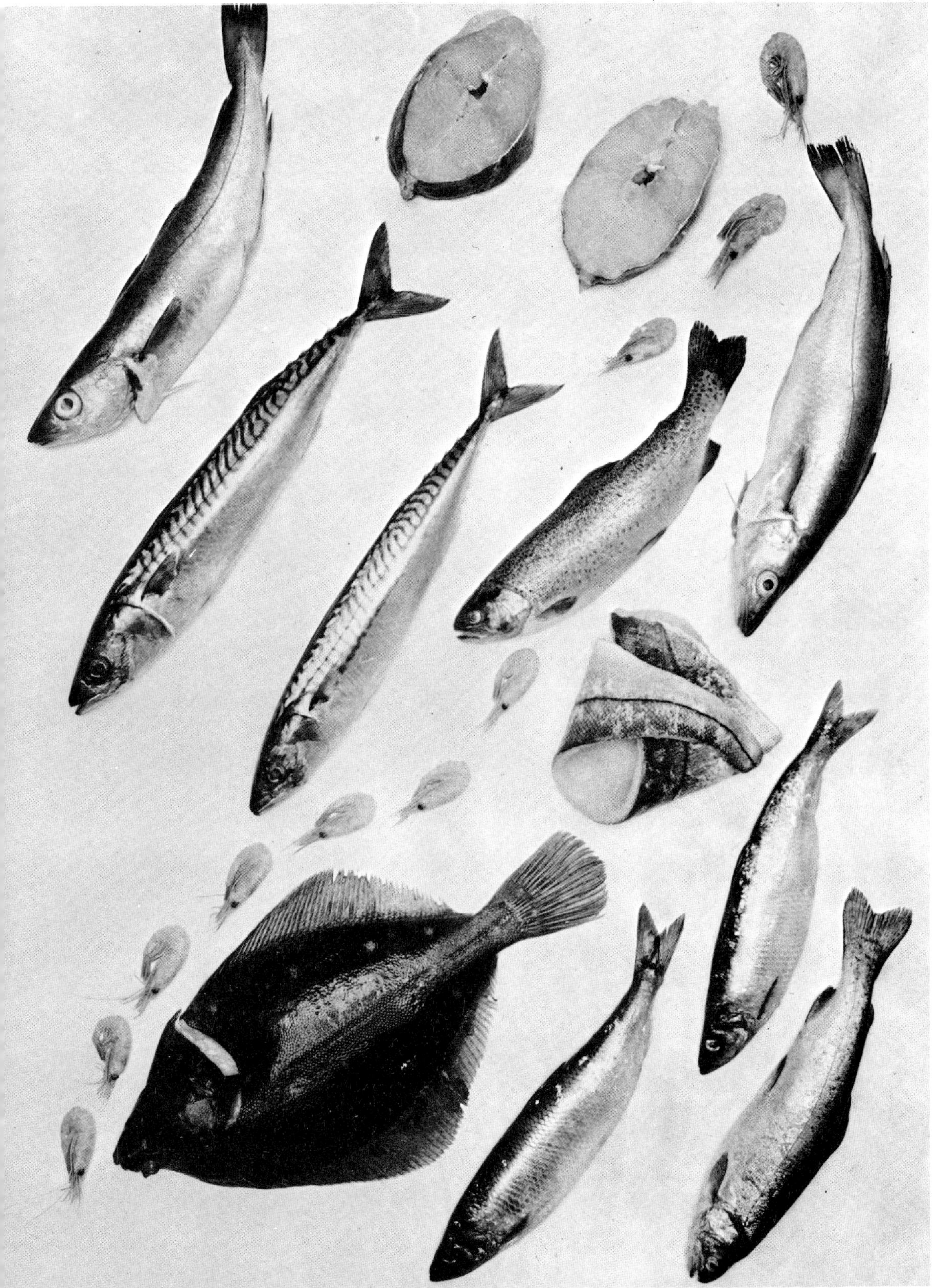

Fish

Fried Fish Fillets

4 fillets of plaice   Breadcrumbs
  or sole   2 oz. dripping or lard
1 egg, beaten   Lemon wedges

Wipe the fillets. Brush them with beaten egg and crumb them, making sure that the coating is firm. Fry the fillets in the hot dripping or lard for 2-3 minutes on each side, or until golden-brown. Drain on crumpled kitchen paper and serve garnished with lemon wedges.

Egging and crumbing, frying and draining the fillets

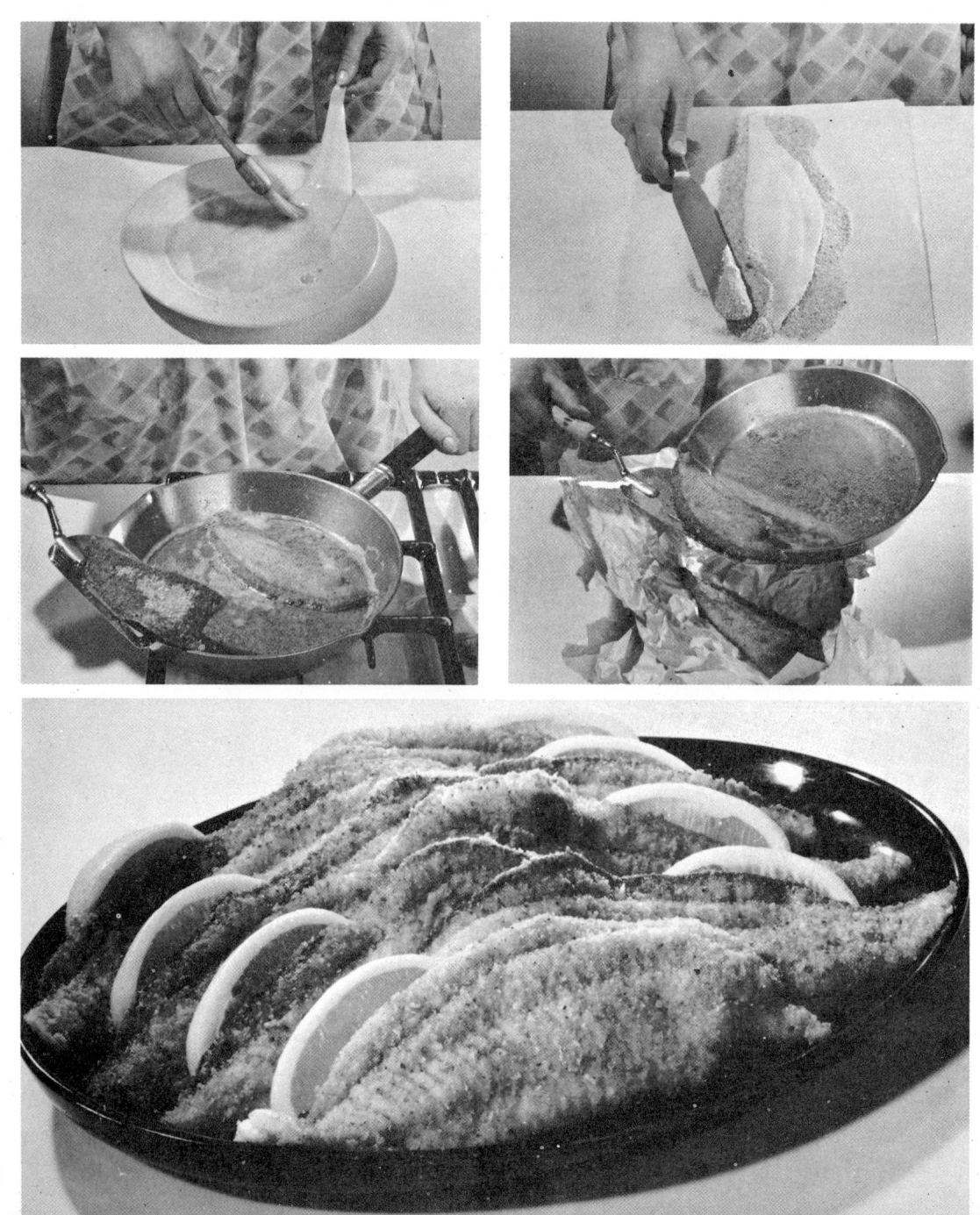

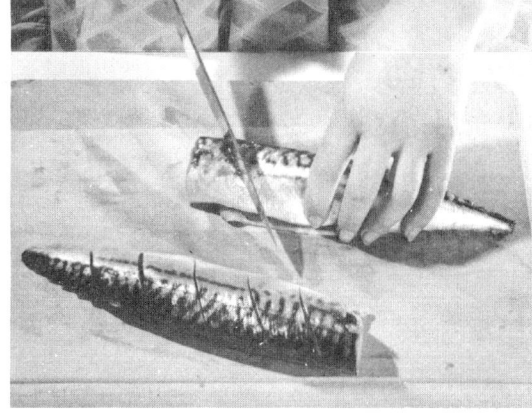

Fried Herrings

| 4 cleaned and filleted herrings | Oatmeal 2 oz. lard or dripping |

Wipe the herrings. Coat them with the oatmeal and fry in the hot lard or dripping until golden-brown, turning them once to ensure that they are evenly cooked—about 5 minutes. Drain well on crumpled kitchen paper.

Grilled Mackerel

Wash 4 mackerel, scrape off the scales and cut off the heads and tails. Slit the underside of the fish and remove the entrails, then wash and dry the fish. Make large slashes at 1-inch intervals and brush with oil. Place the mackerel on the grid of the grill-pan and grill for 8-10 minutes, turning them once during the cooking.

Above: Coating fish with oatmeal; Below: Frying

Above: Slashing the mackerel; Below: Grilling

Fish

Cheesy Grilled Fish

4 cod cutlets
4 oz. Cheddar cheese, grated
½ an onion, grated
3 oz. butter or margarine, softened
Salt and pepper
1 tomato, sliced

Wipe and trim the cutlets. Combine the cheese, onion, butter and seasoning, mixing well. Place the cod steaks on the grill rack and grill lightly on both sides. Spread soft cheese mixture on each cutlet, replace under the grill and cook for 2–3 minutes, or until golden-brown and bubbly. Place a slice of tomato on each cutlet, heat quickly and serve at once. (See colour picture facing page 32.)

Trimming the fish cutlets, grilling, adding the cheese mixture and garnishing

Baked Plaice with Mushrooms

8 fillets of plaice
A squeeze of lemon
  juice
Salt and pepper
2 oz. mushrooms, sliced
1 small onion, finely
  chopped
3 tbsps. milk
1 level tbsp. cornflour
Sprigs of parsley

Heat the oven to fairly hot (375°F., mark 5). Grease an ovenproof dish. Fold each fillet with both ends underneath and place in the dish; squeeze some lemon juice over and season with salt and pepper. Sprinkle the mushrooms and onion on top and add the milk. Bake just above the centre of the oven for 15-20 minutes. Transfer the fillets to a serving dish. Blend the cornflour with the remaining fish liquor and put in a saucepan; bring to the boil and cook for 1 minute. Pour this sauce over the fillets and garnish with parsley.

Cooking the fish and mushrooms, transferring to a serving dish, making and adding the sauce

Fish

Baked Stuffed Fish

4 cod steaks
2 oz. butter
1 oz. fresh breadcrumbs
Grated rind of ½ a lemon
1 level tsp. mixed herbs
Salt and pepper
Milk to mix, if needed
Lemon and parsley garnish

Heat the oven to moderate (350°F., mark 4). Wipe the fish and trim the fins with scissors; cut out the centre bone with a sharp knife. Using a little of the butter, grease an ovenproof dish. Put in the fish. Mix together the breadcrumbs, lemon rind, herbs and seasoning. Melt ½ oz. of the remaining butter and stir into the crumb mixture; mix with a fork and if necessary add a little milk to bind. Divide the stuffing between the fish steaks, filling the holes left by the bones, dot the steaks with the remaining butter and cook on the centre shelf of the oven for about 20 minutes, or until the fish is white and cooked. Serve on a heated dish, garnished with lemon wedges and sprigs of parsley.

Boning the cod steaks, making the stuffing and baking the fish

Grilled Salmon

Though a whole fish or a substantial cut of fresh salmon is usually poached or baked, smaller cutlets or steaks (about 1 inch thick) can be grilled. Brush with melted butter or oil and cook on a greased grid, allowing about 8-10 minutes for each side. Garnish with lemon wedges and parsley and top with a pat of butter.

Baked Salmon

4 salmon cutlets or steaks
2 oz. butter
Salt and pepper
Lemon wedges to garnish

Heat the oven to moderate (350°F., mark 4). Put ½ oz. butter on each cutlet and season it. Cut out 4 squares of foil large enough to enclose a cutlet, place each cutlet on one of the squares and wrap the foil round. Put on a baking sheet and bake for 20 minutes in the centre of the oven. Serve the salmon garnished with lemon wedges and accompanied by green peas.

Baked Salmon: Seasoning the fish and cooking in foil

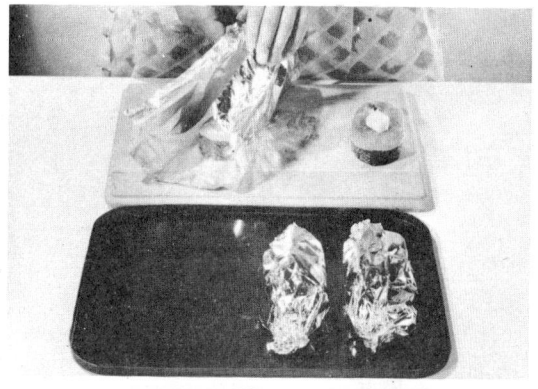

Fish

Fish in Batter

Oil for deep frying
4 pieces of cod fillet
  (or other fish)
Seasoned flour
1 egg
4 oz. flour
$\frac{1}{4}$ pint milk
Lemon wedges

Heat the oil slowly in a deep saucepan. Wipe the fish and toss in seasoned flour. Mix together the egg, flour and half the milk, beat until smooth, then gradually add the rest of the milk, beating all the time. To find out whether the fat is at the correct temperature for frying, put in a 1-inch cube of bread, which should brown in 60 seconds. Coat the fish with the batter and gently lower it into the fat. Fry until golden-brown, then drain on crumpled kitchen paper. Serve with lemon wedges.

Coating the fish with flour and then with batter, deep-frying and draining

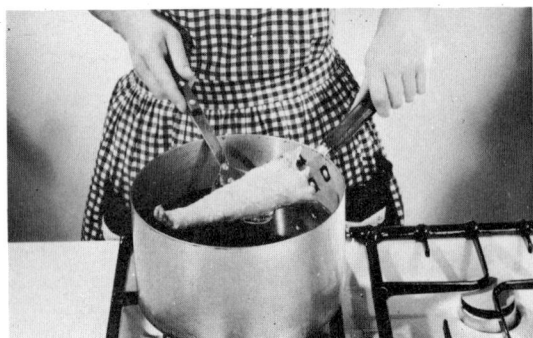

Kedgeree

12 oz. cooked smoked haddock or golden cutlet
2 hard-boiled eggs
3 oz. butter
8 oz. cooked rice
Salt and pepper
Chopped parsley

Remove the skin and bone from the haddock and flake the fish with a fork. Chop one of the hard-boiled eggs and mix with the fish. Melt the margarine in a saucepan and add the rice, fish and egg mixture and seasoning to taste. Stir thoroughly over the heat until the kedgeree is heated through, pile it into a serving dish and garnish with chopped parsley and the remaining egg, cut into neat slices.

Flaking the cooked fish and adding it to the boiled rice

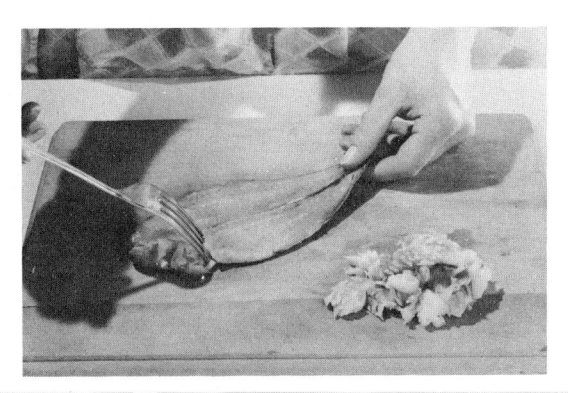

Fish

Preparing Scallops

Scallops, like all shellfish, must be very fresh, so if you are buying them in the shell see that they have bright orange roes and white flesh. Loosen the scallops from the shells with a knife; take off and discard the black part and the beard. Wash the scallops carefully in several changes of water, as they often contain sand or grit, drain and dry them and use as required. Alternatively, buy frozen scallops.

Loosening scallops from shell;
Removing beard; Scallop Fricassee

Scallop Fricassee

6 frozen scallops
Milk
1 oz. butter
1 oz. flour
Seasoning
Lemon wedges and parsley to garnish

Defrost the scallops and cook gently in a little water for about 10 minutes. Drain them, reserving the liquor, and make this up to ½ pint with milk. Keep the scallops hot. Melt the butter in a saucepan and add the flour to make a roux. Gradually add the milk, bring to the boil and cook for 1-2 minutes; season to taste. Arrange the scallops in a dish, pour the sauce over them and garnish with lemon wedges and parsley.

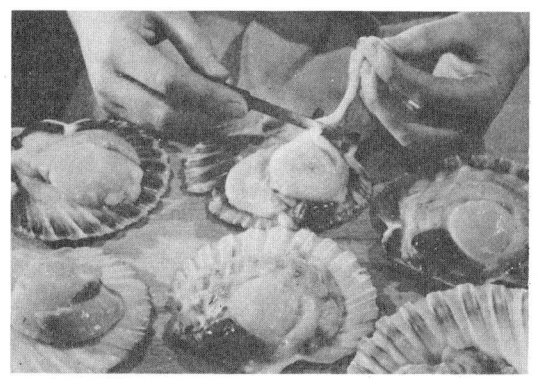

Shredding lettuce and spooning the dressing over the shellfish

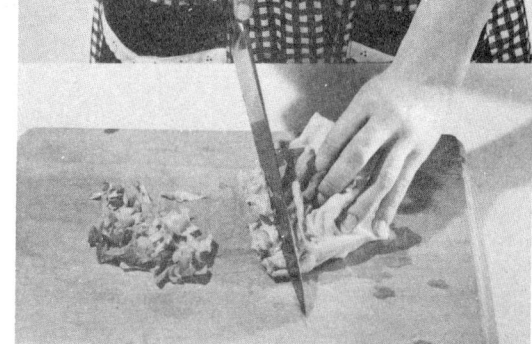

Shellfish Cocktail

4 oz. shellfish	2 tbsps. mayonnaise
1 small lettuce	Seasoning
1 tbsp. cream	Lemon slices to
2 tbsps. tomato ketchup	garnish

Prepare the shellfish as required: crab, lobster, crayfish, prawns and shrimps are all suitable. Shred the lettuce. Mix together the cream, tomato ketchup, mayonnaise and seasoning and mix well. Fill 4 glasses half-full with the shredded lettuce. Pile the shellfish on top, spoon dressing over and garnish with a slice of lemon over the rim of the glass, as seen in the picture.

Fish

Rosy Fish Pie

1 lb. haddock fillets
1 lb. potatoes, peeled
Salt
½ an onion, finely chopped
2 oz. butter or margarine
2 oz. streaky bacon, chopped
2 level tbsps. flour
1 small can of tomatoes
Pepper
2-3 tbsps. milk

Heat the oven to fairly hot (400°F., mark 6). Cut the haddock into 2-inch cubes. Put the potatoes in a saucepan, cover with water, add 1 tsp. salt and bring to the boil; simmer for 20-30 minutes. Fry the onion gently in the hot fat in a shallow pan for 10 minutes—do not let it colour. Add the bacon and fish and cook for a further 5 minutes. Add the flour and blend well, then stir in the tomatoes. Bring to the boil, season and pour into a casserole.

Drain the potatoes and mash with a little milk and seasoning till smooth. Pile the potatoes on top of the fish, level the surface with a knife and mark with a fork. Bake near the top of the oven for ½ hour, until the top is golden-brown.

Above: Cutting up fish; frying onion bacon and fish; transferring fried mixture to casserole; covering with mashed potato
Left: The finished pie

Cheesy Grilled Fish: P. 2

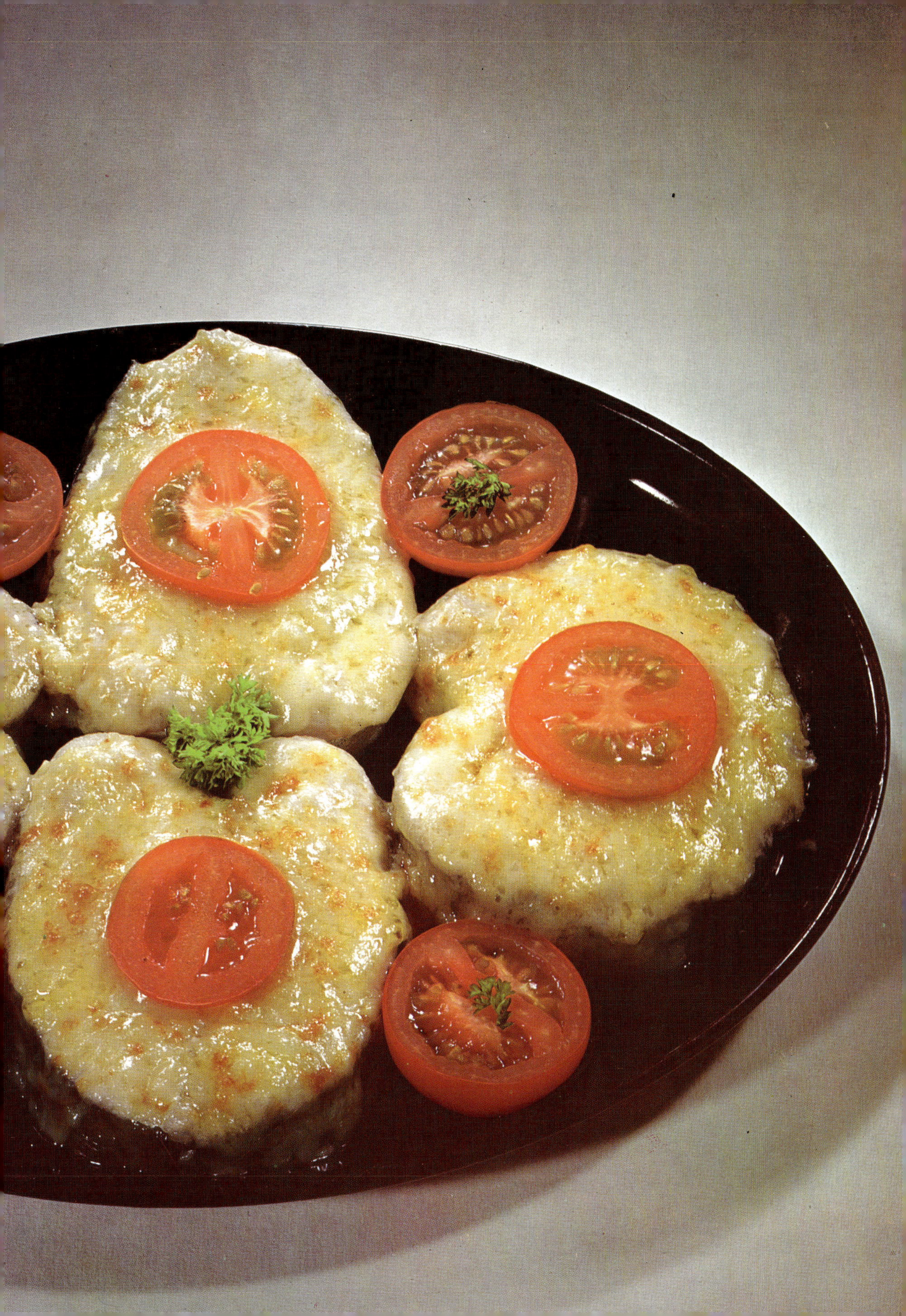

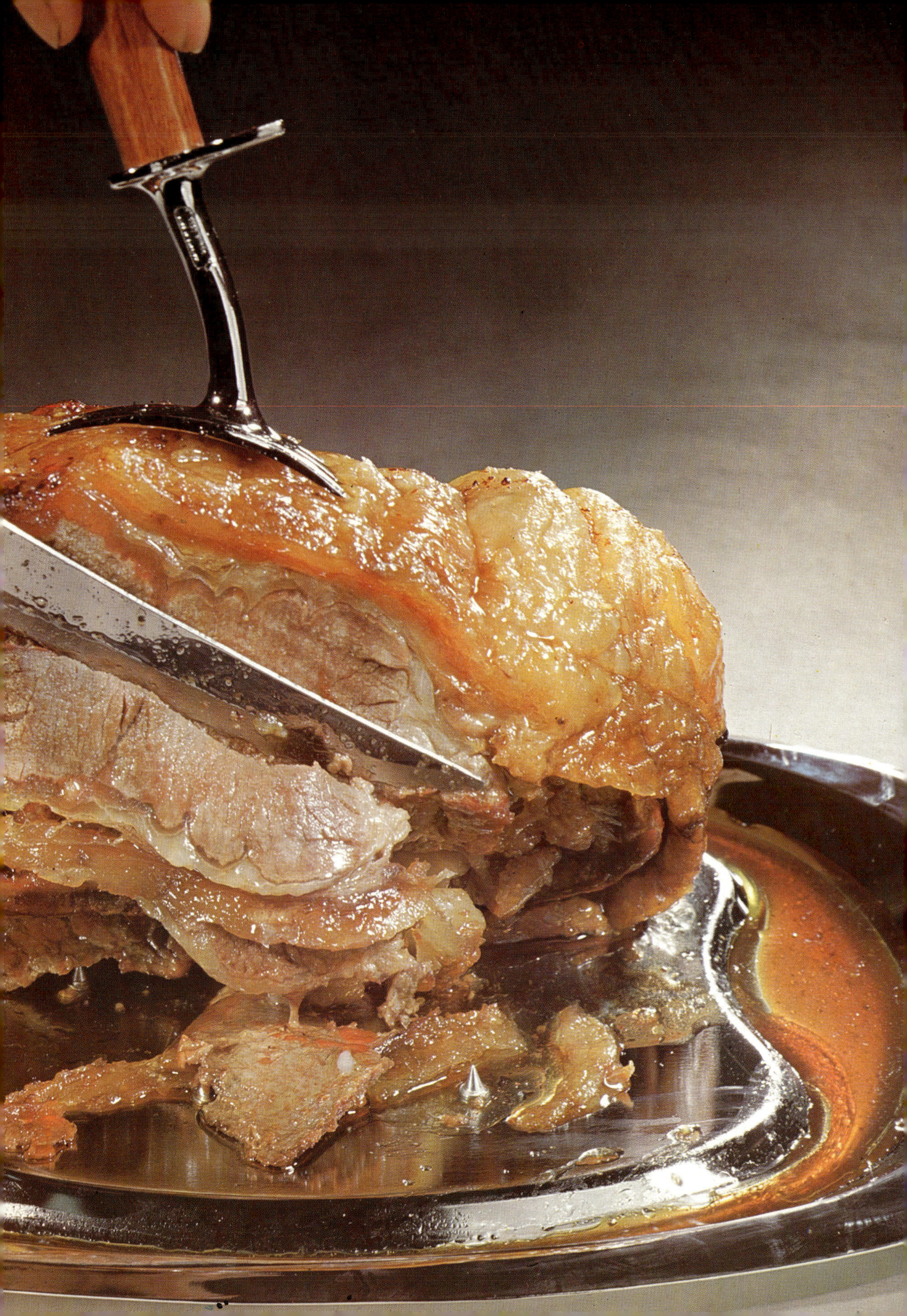

Meat and Poultry

Both meat and poultry may be cooked by almost any method, according to the particular cut or joint. For choice of meat, correct accompaniments, etc., see the pages on Beef, Lamb and so on and also the individual recipes which follow them. (The quantities quoted refer to the raw weight, as purchased.) For gravy-making, see page 88.

ROASTING MEAT

To prepare the joint, wash it, trim or stuff as necessary, then weigh to calculate the cooking time—see below.

1. Quick or High-Temperature

Heat the oven to hot (425°F., mark 7); put the meat in a shallow tin (or on a grid) with the thickest part of any fat uppermost, and bake it in the centre of the oven. Time it as follows:

Beef and Lamb: 15 minutes per lb plus 15 minutes for small or thin joints (e.g., shoulder of lamb); 20 minutes per lb. plus 20 minutes for larger, thicker joints with bone (e.g., sirloin, leg of lamb); 25 minutes per lb. plus 25 minutes for larger joints without bone (e.g., rolled joints).

Pork and Veal: 25 minutes per lb. plus 25 minutes for joints with bone; 30 minutes per lb. plus 30 minutes for boned joints.

2. Slow or Low-Temperature Method

Heat the oven to moderate (350°F., mark 4).

Beef and Lamb: 20 minutes per lb. plus 20 minutes for small joints; 27 minutes per lb. plus 27 minutes for larger joints on the bone; 33 minutes per lb. plus 33 minutes for thick joints off the bone, i.e., rolled.

Pork and Veal: All joints are roasted for 40 minutes per lb. plus 40 minutes.

ROASTING REMINDERS

1. If the meat is lean, place a lump of dripping or lard on it before putting it in the oven, to prevent it drying up.

2. *Basting:* Two or three times during the cooking spoon the juices and fat from the meat over the joint—this keeps it moist and gives a good flavour.

3. You can put fattier joints—especially pork—on a trivet or grid standing in the meat tin, to keep the melted fat away from the meat.

4. Meat can be cooked in a covered roasting tin. This makes the joint more moist and keeps the oven cleaner, though the flavour and colour are not usually quite so good.

5. Roasting in foil makes the meat moist and tender, though here again the flavour is not usually so good. Extra cooking time is not needed, but the foil should be opened out for the final ½ hour, to make the joint brown and crisp.

6. Pork rind should be scored, i.e., cut with a sharp knife, to produce crackling. For a really crisp effect, rub with oil and salt before cooking.

7. Remove any strings either before serving or (if the joint is likely to look untidy) just before carving.

BOILING MEAT

Wipe the meat, place it in a pan with 2 level tsps. salt (unless it is pickled or salted) and add some flavouring ingredients such as 1 onion, 1 carrot, 3 cloves, a bay leaf and a sprig of parsley, then cover with cold water. Bring slowly to boiling point and simmer with the lid on for the required time, as follows:

Fresh Meat, e.g., brisket or silverside of beef, leg of mutton, knuckle of veal: allow 20 minutes per lb. plus 20 minutes.

Salt Meat, e.g., brisket or silverside of beef, belly of pork: allow 25 minutes per lb. plus 25 minutes.

TIME

Below, left to right: Roasting meat on rack; without rack; in covered roasting pan; in aluminium foil

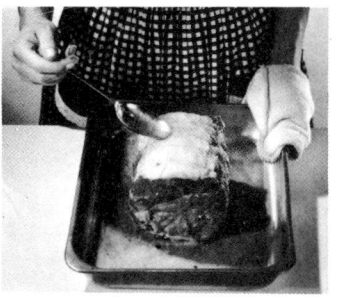

Roast Sirloin of Beef: opposite

Carving Meat

When a joint is well carved it looks attractive and the meat is used in the most economical way. Luckily, carving is an art most people can acquire, given correctly prepared meat and good equipment.

A good butcher will present the joint in the easiest way to carve, if he knows how it is to be served. A joint that includes part of the backbone (e.g., loin) can be "chined"—that is, cut through the ribs close to the backbone, leaving a loose piece of bone that is removed before serving.

When preparing meat for cooking never use wooden skewers, which swell and are difficult to remove.

EQUIPMENT

A long-bladed, sharp knife is essential; steel is usually recommended, as it holds a keen edge. To restore the sharpness, use a steel or a patent sharpener—experienced carvers usually prefer a steel. To use a steel, draw each side of the blade in turn smoothly down and across with rapid strokes, holding the blade at an angle of 45° to the steel. Take great care, if you are a beginner, not to inflict permanent damage on the knife and occasionally, have it expertly reground.

Some modern stainless steel knives have a hollowed-out, grooved blade; these do not often require sharpening and are perhaps easier for an inexperienced person to use, but the skilful carver usually prefers a plain blade.

Keep the carving set separate from other cutlery, or the knife may become dulled.

A sharp two-pronged fork will hold the meat steady; it must have a metal guard to protect the hand in the event of the knife slipping.

A modern meat dish with sharp prongs to hold the joint steady is a great help. Serve the meat with little or no fat and without garnishings. Gravy should be served separately. Place the dish on the table close to the carver and well away from other dishes.

TECHNIQUE

Each joint must be carved in the way best suited to its structure, to ensure a neat result. The carver must understand the make-up of each joint—where the bone is to be found and how the lean and fat are distributed. The meat is usually best when cut across the grain, though sometimes, when the meat is very tender (as in the undercut of sirloin) the joint is cut with the grain.

It is much each easier to carve standing up. Use long, even strokes, keeping the blade at the same angle, to give neat, uniform slices. As you carve, move the knife to and fro, cutting cleanly without bearing down on the meat, which presses out the juices. Serve the carved meat on to very hot plates or it will cool surprisingly quickly.

Beef (except fillet) and veal are carved very thinly (see colour picture facing page 33), but pork and lamb are cut in slices about ¼ inch thick. When cutting a joint with a bone, always take the knife right up to this, so that eventually the bone is left quite clean.

The pictures on pages 35-37 show the carving of a number of joints and we give below notes on the other most familiar types.

Boneless Joints of Beef
Carve across the grain, usually horizontally. In the case of a long piece of roast fillet, however, you will need to carve downwards.

Best End of Neck of Lamb
Cut the joint right through, downwards, into cutlets. (This joint should be chined.)

Saddle of Lamb
First carve the meat from the top of the joint in long slices, cutting downwards and parallel with the backbone. Do this at each side of the bone, then turn the joint and slice the underside.

Leg of Pork
Use the point of the knife to cut through the crackling; it is usually easier to remove it to divide it into portions. Carve as for leg of lamb (see page 36), but medium-thick.

Spare Rib of Pork
Cut between the score marks into moderately thick, even slices.

Stuffed Breast of Lamb or Veal
Cut downwards in fairly thick slices, right through the joint.

Fillet of Veal
The bone is usually removed and replaced by stuffing. Cut across the grain (i.e., horizontally) into medium-thick slices, right across the joint.

If the bone has been left in, cut the meat down to it on one side, then turn the joint over and do the same on the underside.

Sirloin: *Place joint as seen and remove the strings*

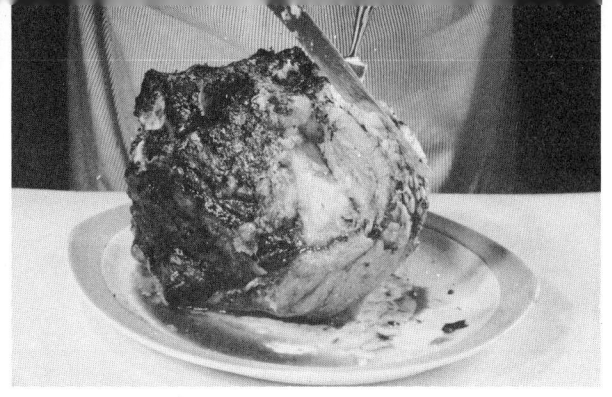

First carve the flank portion into thin slices

Cut fillet, loosening slices from bone with knife-tip

Turn joint over and carve in long slices to the bone

Rib of Beef: *Arrange the joint as seen in the picture*

Slice downwards across the full width of the joint

Cut towards the bone, holding slices with the fork

Slant the slices a little as you continue carving

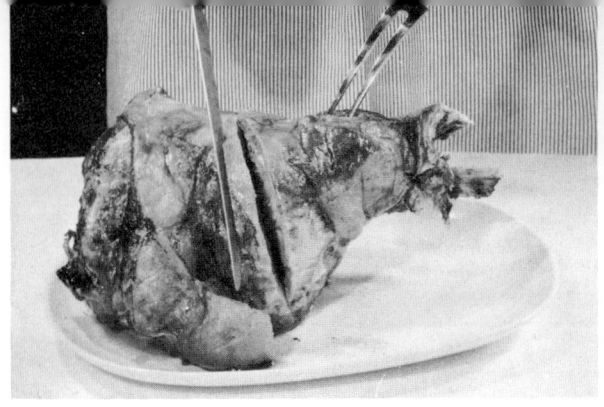

Leg of Lamb: *Begin by cutting 2 wedge-shaped slices*

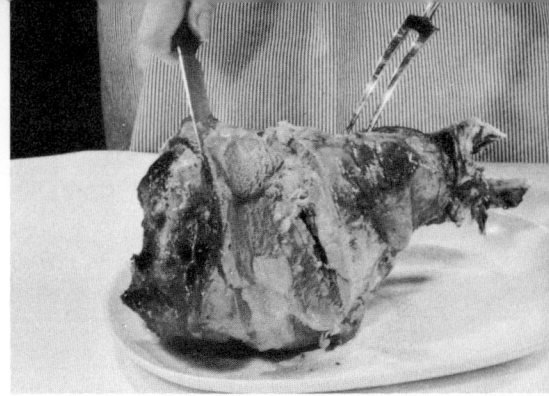

As you carve, turn the knife to get larger slices

Carve down to the bone at other side of the first cut

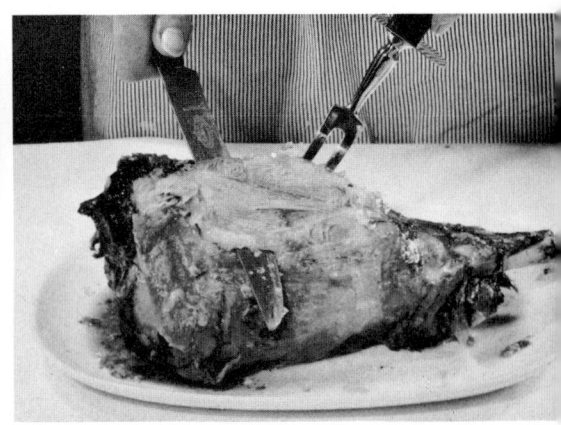

Turn joint over, remove fat and carve long slices

Shoulder of Lamb: *Cut thick slice from the centre*

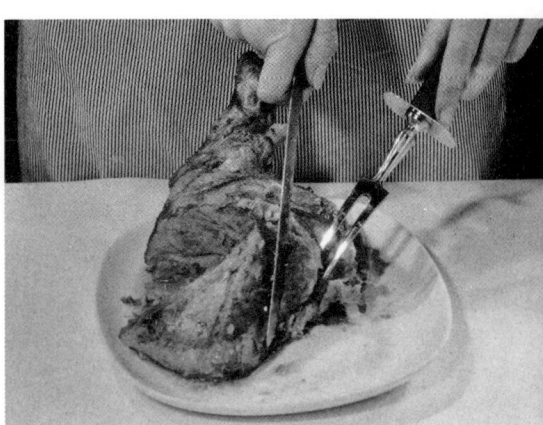

Carve to bone; take small slices from each side of it

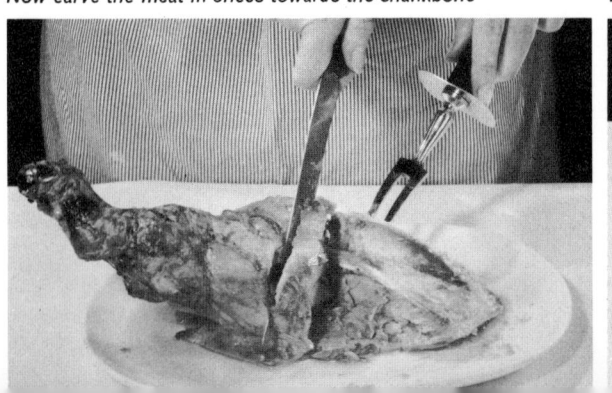

Now carve the meat in slices towards the shankbone

Turn joint over, remove fat and carve in long slices

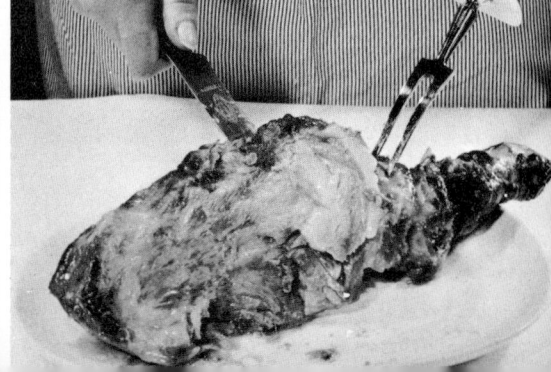

36

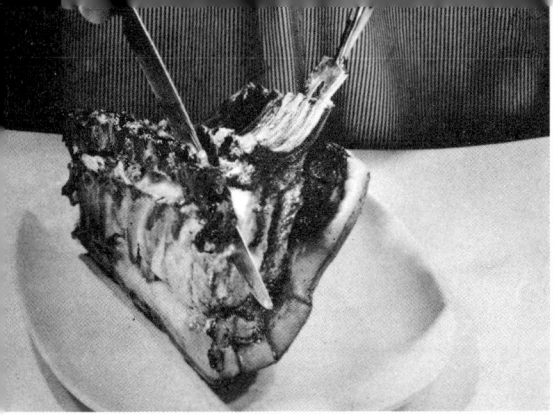

Loin of Pork: *Cut between chined bone and chop bones*

Sever the chined bone and put it to one side of dish

Cut between the bones and the scored crackling

Continue in this way as required to end of joint

Boned and Rolled Pork: *First remove all the strings*

Next cut through the crackling where it was scored

Lift off the crackling and cut into neat portions

Now carve into slices as for any boned rolled joint

Meat and Poultry

Beef

CHOICE

1. The lean should be bright red, the fat creamy to yellow.

2. There should be small flecks of fat through the lean; this fat (called "marbling") helps to keep the lean moist and tender when the meat is cooking.

3. Avoid meat with a line of gristle between lean and fat, which usually suggests it has come from an old animal.

CUTS AND METHOD OF COOKING

Sirloin—a large joint, usually sold on the bone, but it can also be boned and rolled. It is always roasted.
With bone, allow 8-12 oz. per person.
Without bone, allow 6-8 oz. per person.

Rib—a fairly large joint, similar to sirloin; it can be bought on the bone or boned and rolled, and is roasted. Quantities as for sirloin.

Topside—a lean joint, containing no bone, which is therefore economical. It can be roasted in a slow oven, but is often braised.
Allow 6-8 oz. per person.

Brisket—can be sold on or off the bone and is often salted. It is rather a fatty joint, but has a good flavour. Brisket can be slow-roasted or braised; when salted, it should be boiled.
Allow 8-12 oz. per person.

Chuck or Shoulder (known as stewing steak)—a cheaper cut, without bone, fairly lean and suitable for stewing, casseroles, pies and so on.
Allow 6-8 oz. per person.

Leg and Shin—cheap cuts containing a lot of bone, but quite lean and with a good flavour. Long, slow cooking, e.g., stewing, is needed; these cuts can be used for curries, goulash, stews, meat pies and puddings.
Allow 6-8 oz. per person.

ACCOMPANIMENTS

With roast beef serve Yorkshire pudding and horse-radish sauce or mustard.

Rolled Ribs of Beef

Lamb

CHOICE

1. The younger the animal the paler the flesh; in a young lamb it is light pink, while in a mature animal it is light red.

2. A slight blue tinge to the bones suggests the animal is young.

3. Imported lamb has a firm, white fat, while English lamb (only available in spring and early summer) has creamy-coloured fat.

Lamb, whether imported or home-produced, is probably the most consistent meat available as regards quality and price.

CUTS AND METHOD OF COOKING

Loin—a prime cut, usually roasted; can be cooked on or off the bone; if boned, it is often stuffed and rolled.
Allow 8-12 oz. on the bone per person.

Leg—another good roasting cut.
Allow 12 oz. on the bone per person. The meat is often sold cut from the bone for use in pies, stews, kebabs and so on.

Shoulder—a large joint, with more fat but often with more flavour than leg. Usually roasted. Shoulder meat can also be sold off the bone, as for leg.
Allow 12 oz. on the bone per person.

Chops—these can be cut from the loin, those with a small amount of bone being known as chump chops. Suitable for grilling, frying and casseroles.
Allow 1-2 per person.

Cutlets—these have a small 'eye' of lean meat and a long bone; suitable for grilling or frying.
Allow 1-2 per person.

Breast—a rather fatty cut, therefore usually quite cheap. Usually boned, stuffed and rolled; it can be braised, slow-roasted or stewed.
Allow 8-12 oz. on the bone per person.

Middle and Scrag End—cheap cuts with rather a high proportion of bone and fat, but with a good flavour. Suitable for stews and casseroles.
Allow 12 oz. per person.

ACCOMPANIMENTS

With roast lamb and grilled chops, serve mint sauce or jelly; with roast mutton, red-currant jelly and onion sauce are sometimes served.

With boiled leg of mutton, caper sauce is traditional.

Roast Leg of Lamb

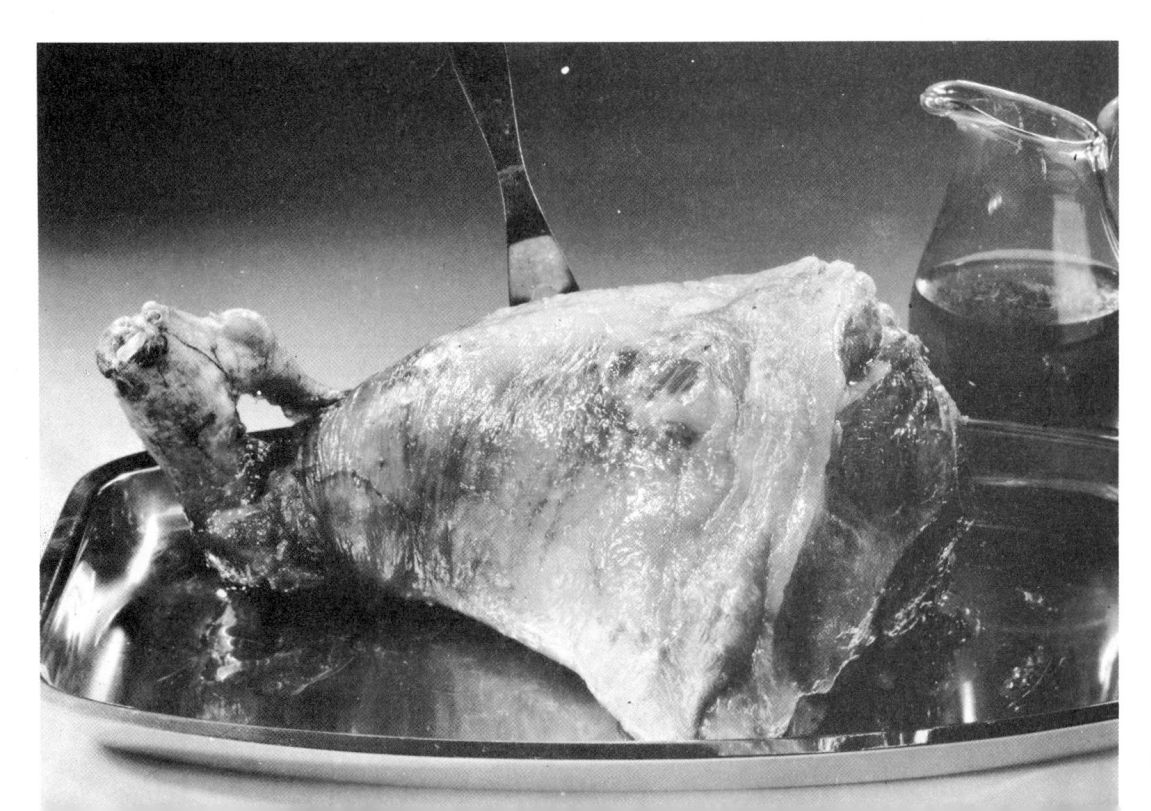

Meat and Poultry

Pork

CHOICE

1. Pork should have pale pink, moist lean, which should be slightly marbled with fat.

2. There should be a good outer layer of firm, white fat, with a thin, elastic skin.

3. The bones should be small and pinkish—denoting a young animal.

4. Although pork was considered seasonal at one time, it can now quite safely be bought all the year round; prices, however, vary considerably, so check up before buying.

CUTS & METHODS OF COOKING

Fillet—a lean, fairly expensive cut, with a central bone. It is best roasted and can be cooked on the bone or boned and stuffed. This cut is also sold as fairly thin slices and is then grilled, fried or casseroled.
Allow 8-12 oz. on the bone per person.

Loin—an expensive but very prime cut, suitable for roasting; it often includes the kidney. It can be cooked on the bone or boned and stuffed.
Allow 8-12 oz. on the bone per person.

Spare Rib—fairly lean and moderately priced. Good for roasting, but can also be cut up for braising and stewing.
Allow 8-12 oz. on the bone per person.

Chops—usually consist of the cut-up loin and often include the kidney. They are more expensive than chops from other meat. They can be grilled, fried or casseroled.
Allow 1 per person.

Cutlets—these are cut from the spare-rib and have little or no bone; they are usually lean. Cutlets are cooked as chops.
Allow 1-2 per person.

Blade—another cut for roasting on the bone.
Allow 8-12 oz. on the bone per person.

Belly—a fatty cut, sometimes sold salted; usually boiled and served cold.
Allow 4-6 oz. per person.

ACCOMPANIMENTS

Apple sauce is the most usual accompaniment, with sage and onion stuffing, if this is liked. Any extra stuffing can be made into small balls and cooked in a tin in the oven.

Roast Loin of Pork

Bacon and Gammon

CHOICE

These can be bought in the piece and either boiled or baked to serve as a joint. Joints of bacon suitable for boiling are back, streaky, collar and hock; those suitable for baking are collar and hock.

Gammon is sold as slipper, hock, middle and corner gammon; all are suitable for either boiling or baking. Allow 4-6 oz. per person.

To Boil Bacon or Gammon

Weigh the piece, then calculate the cooking time. Tie it if necessary to keep it a good shape. Cover it with water and allow to soak for about 1 hour. Place the joint in a large pan and cover with fresh cold water, bring to the boil, then simmer gently until cooked, allowing 20-25 minutes per lb., plus 20 minutes over. If you are cooking a large joint, e.g., a gammon of 10 lb. or over, allow 15-20 minutes per lb., plus 15 minutes over.

When the joint is cooked, remove the skin with a knife, if necessary, and serve the meat hot, with parsley sauce.

Alternatively, allow the joint to cool in the cooking liquid, cut off the outer skin and press browned breadcrumbs into the fat; when the meat is cold, serve with salad or in sandwiches.

To Bake Gammon or Bacon

After weighing the meat and calculating the cooking time, soak as for boiled bacon. Boil for half the cooking time, then drain the joint and wrap in foil. Bake in a moderate oven (350°F., mark 4) until ½ hour before the cooking time is completed. Raise the oven heat to hot (425°F., mark 7).

Put 2-3 tbsps. brown sugar, 1 oz. butter and 1 tbsp. water in a small saucepan, dissolve and bring to the boil. Undo the foil round the bacon, cut off the skin and brush the surface with the sugar glaze; return the joint to the oven and leave until crisp and golden. Serve with cranberry sauce or with canned pineapple, peaches or apricots.

Boiled Bacon: Picture 1—lowering joint into pan of water; picture 2, removing skin. Baked Bacon (bottom picture) served with pineapple

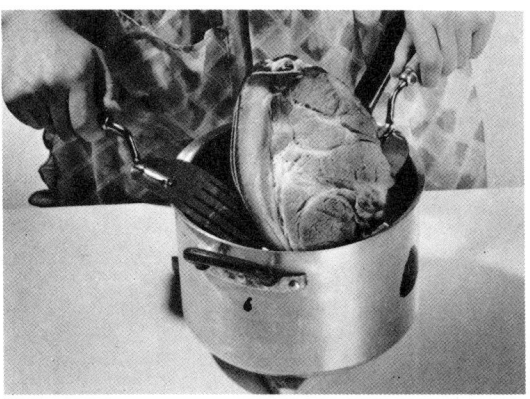

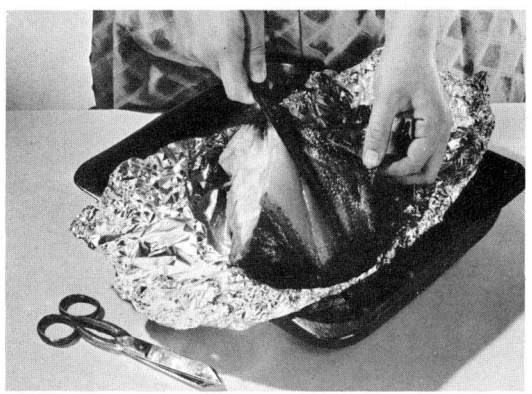

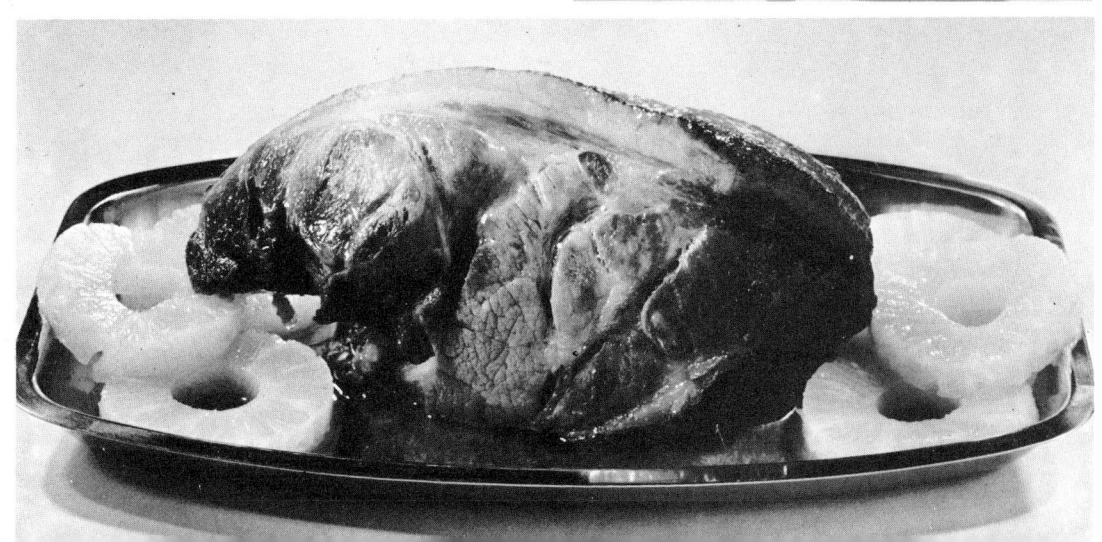

Meat and Poultry

Grilled Steak

4 steaks
¼ lb. mushrooms
4 tomatoes
Butter
Salt and pepper
Oil

Trim the steaks. Peel the mushrooms, halve the tomatoes and put a small knob of butter on each half. Season the mushrooms and tomatoes with salt and pepper. Brush the steaks with oil, season with salt and pepper and cook them under a hot grill for 5-7 minutes for rare steak, 10-12 minutes medium and 15 minutes well done, turning them frequently. Lightly grill mushrooms and tomatoes and arrange with steaks on a serving dish.

Below: Peeling mushrooms, brushing steak with oil; steaks served with mushrooms and tomatoes

Grilled Pork Chops with Apple Rings

4 pork chops
Olive oil
1 large apple, peeled and cut in round slices

Trim the chops, place on the grid of the grill and brush with oil. Core the apple slices. Grill the chops for 7-10 minutes on each side under a medium grill, to make sure that they are well cooked. When they are done, place on a serving dish and keep hot. Put the apple rings on the grid and brown very lightly. Arrange between the chops on a serving dish.

Below: Brushing chops with oil; coring apple slices; chops dished up with apple

Meat and Poultry

Beef Stew

1½ lb. stewing steak 1½ oz. flour
2 tbsps. oil 1½ pints stock
2 onions, sliced Seasoning
2-3 carrots, sliced A bouquet garni

Heat the oven to moderate (350°F., mark 4). Cut the meat into cubes. Heat the oil in a shallow pan and sauté the onions and carrots until golden-brown; remove from the pan. Sauté the meat until well browned. Place the meat and vegetables in a casserole. Add the flour to the fat remaining in the pan and make a roux. Add the stock gradually, bring to the boil, season and add the bouquet garni. Pour into the casserole and cook in the centre of the oven for 2-2½ hours. Remove the bouquet garni before serving. This type of dish is sometimes called a "brown stew".

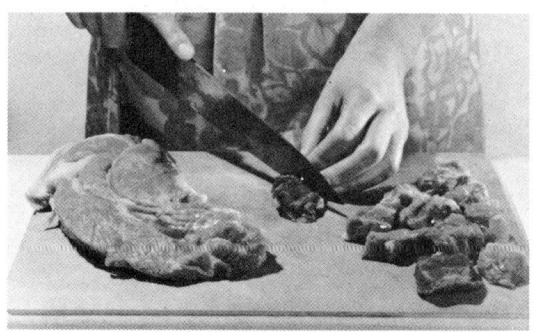

Below: Cutting up beef; slicing onions; adding sautéed meat to casserole; pouring in thickened stock; the finished beef stew ready to serve

Irish Stew

1 lb. middle neck of mutton
2 lb. potatoes, peeled
3 onions, peeled
Seasoning
Stock

Heat the oven to moderate (350°F., mark 4). Cut up the meat. Slice the potatoes and onions. Place alternating layers of meat, potato and onion in a casserole, finishing with a layer of potato. Season well and add enough stock to half-cover. Place in the centre of the oven and cook for 2-2½ hours. If liked, garnish with chopped parsley before serving.

Cutting up mutton; slicing potatoes and onions; pouring in stock; the cooked Irish stew

Meat and Poultry

Veal Stew

1 lb. pie veal
2 onions, chopped
2 carrots, sliced
4 oz. mushrooms, peeled and sliced
¾ pint stock
A bouquet garni
Seasoning
1 level tbsp. cornflour

Heat the oven to moderate (350°F., mark 4). Cut the meat into small pieces and place in a casserole with the onions, carrots and mushrooms. Pour on the stock, add the bouquet garni and season well. Cook towards the bottom of the oven for about 1 hr. Strain off the liquor, blend with the cornflour and put into a saucepan; heat, stirring, until thickened, then add to the veal and heat through. Turn the stew into a dish or serve in the casserole.

Below: Preparing the ingredients; pouring in the thickened stock; the cooked veal stew

Summer Stew

1 lb. middle neck of mutton
½ a bunch of young carrots
2 onions
½ lb. small turnips
1 lb. small new potatoes
1 lb. unshelled peas or small packet frozen peas
Salt and pepper
2 level tbsps. chopped mint
2 level tbsps. chopped parsley

Trim the meat and prepare the vegetables, leaving them whole. Place the meat, carrots, onions and turnips in a large saucepan. Just cover with water and simmer for ½–¾ hour. Add the potatoes, peas, seasoning, mint and parsley and continue to cook for another hour, or until the meat and vegetables are tender. Re-season if necessary and place in a serving dish.

Preparing the meat and the vegetables, pouring in the water and adding the mint and parsley

Meat and Poultry

Lancashire Hot-Pot

1 lb. chuck or shoulder steak
Seasoned flour
4 medium-sized onions, peeled
1½ lb. potatoes, peeled
Salt and pepper
¾ pint beef stock
A knob of butter

Heat the oven to warm (325°F., mark 3). Cut the meat into 1-inch cubes and toss in seasoned flour. Slice the onions and potatoes. Place a layer of meat in the casserole, cover with a layer of onions and potatoes and season. Repeat, finishing with a layer of potatoes. Add the stock, season well, dot with butter and cover. Cook in the centre of the oven for 2½-3 hours. Remove the lid ½ hour before the end of the cooking, to brown the potatoes.

Cubing the meat, slicing the onions, layering the ingredients in the casserole and dotting with butter

Meat Loaf

1 tbsp. oil
1 onion, finely chopped
½ lb. minced beef
½ lb. sausage-meat
1 oz. fresh breadcrumbs
1 level tsp. mixed herbs
Salt and pepper
1 egg, beaten

Heat the oven to moderate (350°F., mark 4). Grease a 1-lb. loaf tin. Heat the oil in a shallow pan and fry the chopped onion until it is light golden-brown. Combine the minced beef, sausage-meat, breadcrumbs, herbs and seasoning with the beaten egg and mix till smooth. Place this mixture in the prepared tin, cover with greased greaseproof paper and cook for ¾-1 hour. Allow the loaf to cool in the tin, turn out and slice before serving.

Mixing the ingredients for meat loaf; putting into the tin; serving with pickled onions

Meat and Poultry

Liver Casserole

2 oz. lard or dripping
1 lb. liver, sliced
Seasoned flour
6 rashers of bacon, chopped
4 onions, sliced
1 medium can of tomatoes
1 tbsp. Worcestershire sauce
Salt and pepper

Heat the oven to moderate (350°F., mark 4). Heat the fat. Toss the liver in the seasoned flour. Sauté the liver, bacon and onions until golden-brown. Transfer them to a casserole and add the tomatoes, Worcestershire sauce and seasoning. Cook in the centre of the oven for 45 minutes, or until the liver is tender.

Sautéing the liver, bacon and onions; adding the canned tomatoes; the finished liver casserole

Baked Stuffed Liver

1 lb. lamb's liver, sliced ½-inch thick
4 oz. bacon, rinded
½ pint stock

For the Stuffing
4 oz. fresh breadcrumbs
1 small onion, chopped finely
1 level tsp. mixed herbs
1 oz. margarine, melted
1 egg, beaten

Heat the oven to moderate (350°F., mark 4). Prepare the stuffing in the same way as Forcemeat (see page 90). Place the liver in a greased ovenproof dish. Spread some stuffing on each piece of liver, then top with a piece of bacon (short back or streaky). Pour in the stock and cover.

Bake in the centre of the oven for 45 minutes, removing the covering during the last 10 minutes of the time, to crisp the bacon rashers.

Layering the liver with the stuffing and bacon and pouring in the stock

Meat and Poultry

Steak and Mushroom Pie

1½ lb. chuck or shoulder steak	4 oz. mushrooms, sliced
Seasoned flour	½ pint stock or water
1 onion, chopped	1 pkt. bought puff pastry
	Beaten egg to glaze

Cut the meat in 1-inch cubes and toss them in the flour. Put the meat, onion and mushrooms in a pan, add just sufficient liquid to cover, put on lid and cook gently over a low heat until tender—about 1½ hours. Cool. Heat the oven to hot (425°F., mark 7). Transfer the meat, etc., to a pie dish, with enough gravy to half-cover. Roll out the thawed pastry and cut off a thin strip for edge of pie. Damp rim of dish, stick on the pastry strip and put on the top, then seal and decorate the edges. Brush pastry with a little egg. Bake pie for 30 minutes at top of oven.

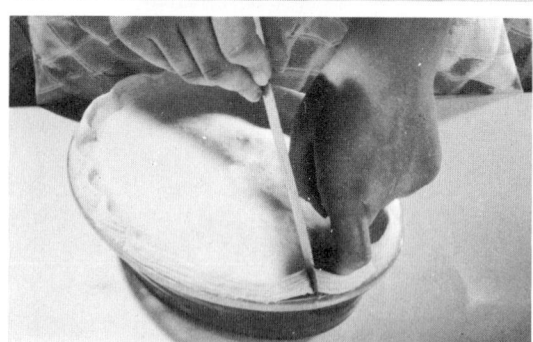

Putting pre-cooked meat and mushrooms into dish, covering with pastry and decorating the edges

Meat Pasties

8 oz. minced beef
1 medium onion, chopped
1 tbsp. oil
2 tomatoes, skinned and chopped
1-2 level tsps. chopped parsley
1 tsp. Worcestershire sauce
Salt and pepper
1 pkt. bought puff pastry
1 egg, beaten

Heat the oven to hot (425°F., mark 7). Fry the beef and onion in the oil until the meat is well browned. Add the tomatoes, parsley, sauce and seasoning and keep hot. Roll out the pastry into a large square and divide into 4 squares, each 6 by 6 inches. Spoon a little of the meat filling on one half of a square, brush the edges with a little beaten egg and fold the other half of the pastry over the filling, as seen in the photograph. Seal the edges well and flake them with a round-bladed knife, repeat for the other squares. Place the pasties on a greased and floured baking sheet and make a small slit in the top of each. Brush the tops with the remaining egg and bake just above the centre of the oven for 20-25 minutes, until the pastry is well risen and golden-brown.

Preparing filling; cutting pastry into 4 squares; adding filling; folding pastry over

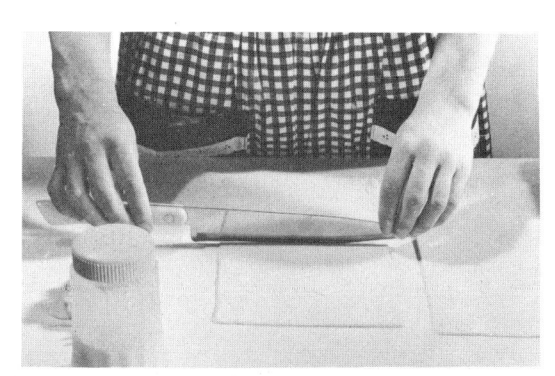

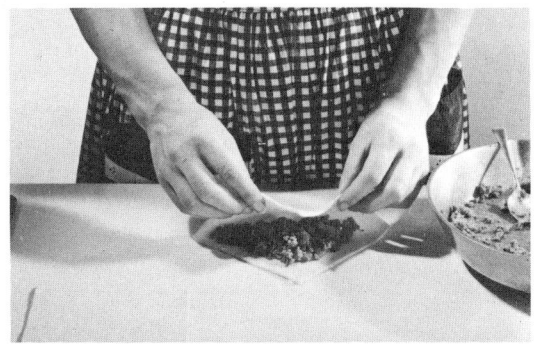

Meat and Poultry

Bacon Roly-Poly

8 oz. suetcrust pastry
6 oz. bacon, finely chopped
2 oz. minced beef
1 small onion, finely chopped
1 level tsp. chopped parsley
½ level tsp. mixed herbs
1-2 tbsps. stock to moisten
Salt and pepper

Put some water in a steamer and bring to the boil. Make the suetcrust pastry (see page 110) and roll it out to an oblong 12 by 6 inches. Mix the remaining ingredients and spread this filling on the pastry to within ¼ inch of each edge, then roll the pastry up to form a roll. Wrap in a sheet of greased greaseproof paper and secure the ends firmly. Wrap in a cloth and steam over fast-boiling water for 2½-3 hours.

Rolling out pastry; mixing and adding filling; wrapping roly-poly in greaseproof paper

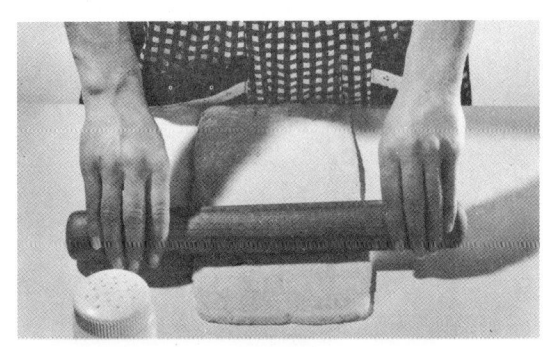

Steak and Kidney Pudding

8 oz. suetcrust pastry
1 lb. stewing steak, chopped small
2 lamb's kidneys' chopped small
1 level tbsp. flour
1 level tsp. salt
A dash of pepper
1 small onion, chopped
A little stock

Put some water in a steamer and bring to the boil. Grease a 6-inch pudding basin. Make the suetcrust pastry (see page 110). Roll the pastry out into a round and cut out a quarter of it to keep for the top. Line the pudding basin with the rest—avoid stretching it. Toss the meat and kidney in the seasoned flour. Mix with the onion and put into the basin. Pour in the stock. Roll out the remaining pastry into a round, place on the basin and seal carefully. Cover with greased foil and secure with string, then steam for 3-4 hours over fast-boiling water. Serve with a napkin tied round the basin.

Cutting off pastry for "lid"; adding meat; putting on pastry top; covering with foil

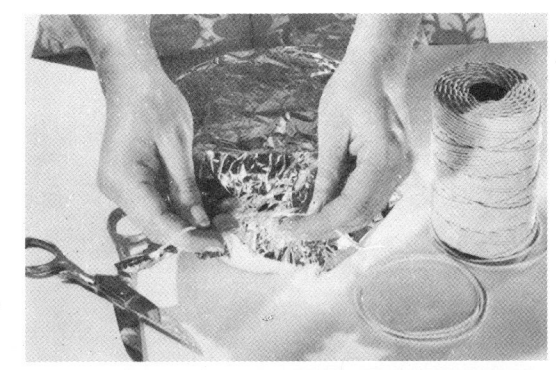

Meat and Poultry

Curried Beef

1 lb. stewing steak	Salt and pepper
2 oz. lard	1 level tbsp. chutney
1 cooking apple, chopped	2 oz. sultanas
2 large onions, chopped	2 tomatoes, skinned and quartered
1 level tbsp. curry paste	
3 level tbsp. flour	A squeeze of lemon juice
1 pint stock or water	Boiled rice

Cut the meat into cubes. Heat the fat in a thick-based saucepan and fry the chopped apple and onions until golden. Add the meat and fry, stirring all the time, until it is browned. Add the curry paste and flour and fry for 2-3 minutes. Gradually add the stock, stir well and boil for 2-3 minutes. Add the seasoning, chutney, sultanas, tomatoes and a squeeze of lemon juice. Cover with a close-fitting lid and simmer gently over a low heat for 2-2½ hours, or cook in a moderate oven (350°F., mark 4), stirring occasionally to prevent the curry sticking to the base of the pan. Before serving, adjust the seasoning as required and place the curry on a hot dish, with a border of boiled rice. Chutney may, be served as an accompaniment.

Raw poultry, various meats and vegetables may also be curried in this way. When making a curry of cooked meat, poultry, eggs or vegetables, or of white fish (which requires less cooking), make the curry sauce, cook it for the full time to blend the flavours, then add the cooked food and heat it in the sauce for about 10-15 minutes.

Success in curry-making depends on the blending of all the flavours during the long, slow cooking, so that no one of them predominates in the final result. A curry is not therefore a dish to make when you are in a hurry.

Curried Mince

1 lb. lean beef
1½ oz. dripping or lard
2 medium-sized onions, chopped
1 large cooking apple, finely chopped
1 level tbsp. curry paste
1 level tbsp. flour
½ pint stock
1 level tbsp. chutney
2 oz. sultanas
Cooked rice
Lemon wedges to garnish

Mince the beef (or get the butcher to do this when you buy it). Heat the dripping and lightly fry the onions and apple until golden-brown; remove from the pan and put into a saucepan. To the remaining fat add the curry paste and flour to make a roux; gradually add the stock, bring to the boil and cook for 1-2 minutes. Stir in the chutney and sultanas, then add to the saucepan and simmer for 20-30 minutes. Fry the mince in the remaining ½ oz. fat and add to the sauce. Continue to simmer for 15 minutes. Serve in a shallow dish, with a border of cooked rice and lemon wedges to garnish.

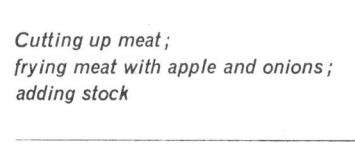

*Cutting up meat;
frying meat with apple and onions;
adding stock*

Putting the fried onions and apple into the pan; adding the fried mince; putting the curry into a rice border

Meat and Poultry

Roast Chicken

1 frozen chicken (about 3lb.) 2 rashers of bacon

Sage and onion stuffing Fat for roasting
 (see page 90)

Thaw out the bird and remove the giblets from the inside. Heat the oven to fairly hot (400°F., mark 6). Stuff the chicken and fold the skin round the neck opening under the wing tips; tie the legs firmly and place 2 rashers of bacon over the breast. Place in a roasting tin with some fat. Cook in the centre of the oven for about an hour, or until done, basting every 15 minutes; 15 minutes before the end of the cooking, remove the bacon. Take the string from the legs before serving. Put the bird on a dish and garnish with watercress; serve bread sauce separately.

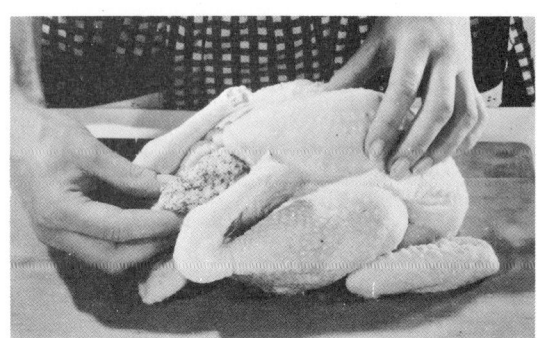

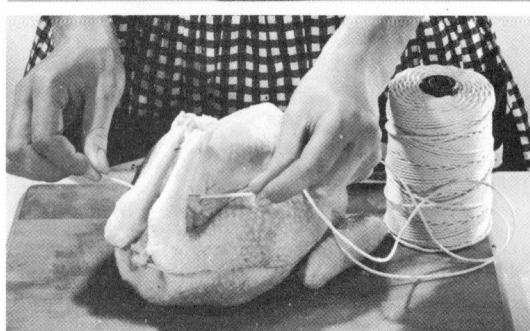

Removing the giblets from the ready-cleaned bird; stuffing the chicken; tucking the neck flap under the wing tips; trussing the bird

Baked Chicken Joints

4 oz. butter (or 2 oz. butter and 2 tbsps. oil)
4 chicken joints
1 egg, beaten
Fresh breadcrumbs
1 small raw onion, cut into rings (optional)

Heat the oven to fairly hot (400°F., mark 6). Melt the butter in a roasting tin. Coat the chicken joints with the egg and toss them in the fresh crumbs. Place the joints in the melted fat and bake towards the top of the oven for 30 minutes, turn them over and bake for a further 20 minutes. When the joints are golden-brown, remove from the tin and drain on crumpled kitchen paper. Arrange on a serving dish and garnish with rings of raw onion.

Coating the chicken with beaten egg;
putting into the tin;
turning and draining the pieces

Vegetables

Potatoes

Boiled—if the potatoes are old, wash them well, then peel thinly with a knife or potato peeler and cut into even-sized pieces. If new, wash and scrape. As soon as they have been prepared, put them into cold water until wanted for cooking, to prevent their discolouring. Put into salted water and simmer until cooked but unbroken—15-20 minutes for new potatoes, 20-30 minutes for old ones. Drain well, toss with a knob of butter and serve sprinkled with chopped parsley.

Mashed—prepare and boil some old potatoes as above. Drain well, then mash with a potato masher or fork, until quite free from lumps.

Creamed—mash the potatoes as above, then add a knob of butter, 3-4 tbsps. milk and a little extra seasoning if necessary. Return them to the heat and beat well with a wooden spoon until smooth, creamy and really white. Pile into a dish, mark the top with a fork and serve sprinkled with chopped parsley.

Baked in their Jackets—choose even-sized old potatoes. Scrub well and prick all over with a fork. Bake near the top of a fairly hot oven (400°F., mark 6) for about ¾-1 hour, or until they feel soft when squeezed. Cut a cross in the top of each potato, put in a knob of butter and serve at once.

Roast—choose old potatoes. Wash, peel and cut into even-sized pieces. Cook in salted water for 5-10 minutes (depending on size). Drain well, then carefully transfer to a Yorkshire pudding tin or shallow cake tin, containing 4 oz. of hot lard or dripping. Baste well and bake near the top of a hot oven (425°F., mark 7) for 20 minutes, then turn them and continue cooking for a further 20 minutes or until tender inside and crisp and brown outside. Drain well on crumpled kitchen paper, put into an uncovered serving dish, sprinkle with salt and serve at once. If preferred, the potatoes need not be par-boiled first (in this case they will take 50-60 minutes to cook); they may also be cooked in the roasting tin around the meat, when little or no extra fat will be needed.

Chipped—choose old potatoes; wash and peel them, then cut into ¼-½ inch slices. Cut these slices into long strips ¼-½ inch wide. (Several slices can be put on top of one another and cut together for speed.) Put some fat in a deep saucepan or fryer and heat until when one chip is dropped into the fat, it rises to the surface straight away, surrounded by bubbles. Put the remaining chips into the basket and lower into the fat; cook until golden and tender inside. Drain well on crumpled kitchen paper and serve straight away in an uncovered dish.

Sauté (Fried)—cut cold boiled potatoes into rounds ¼ inch thick and fry in a little hot lard, turning once, until crisp and golden on both sides. Drain well on crumpled kitchen paper and serve at once, sprinkled with chopped parsley.

Pictures opposite show, from top to bottom: Draining and mashing potatoes; Preparing and serving creamed potatoes; Pricking potatoes to bake in their jackets and adding butter; Cooking and draining roast potatoes; Preparing chipped potatoes; Cooking sauté potatoes

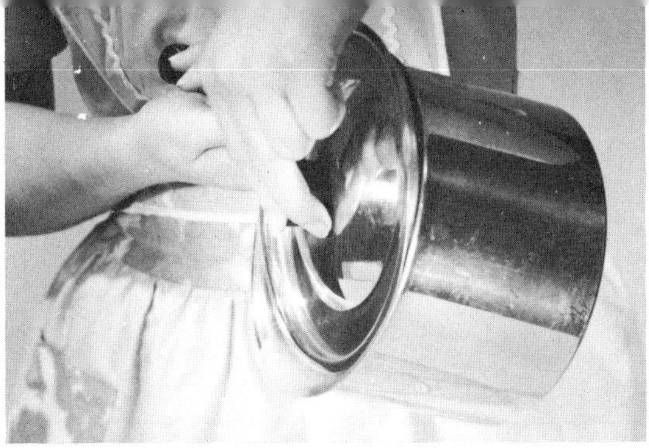
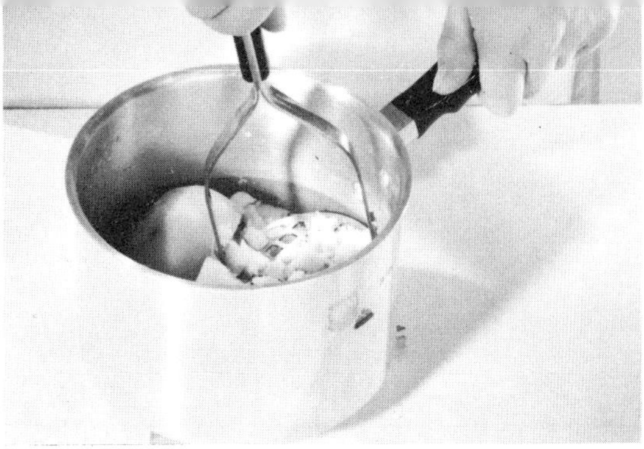
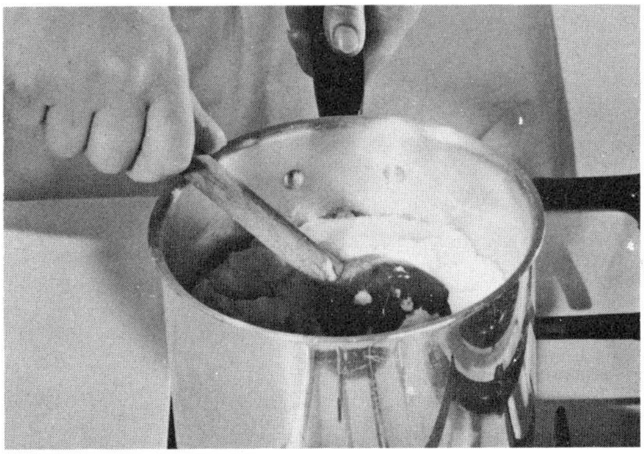
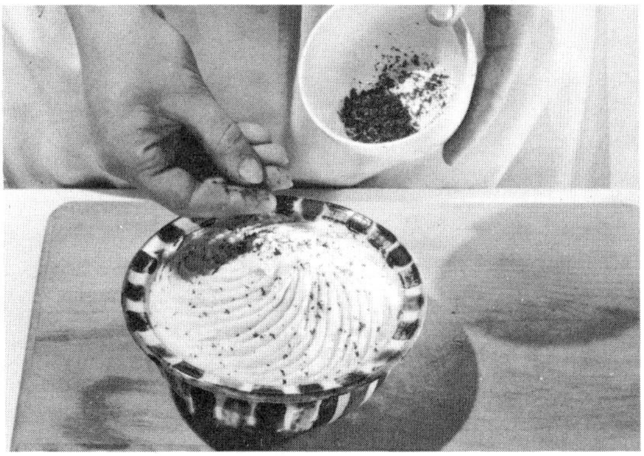
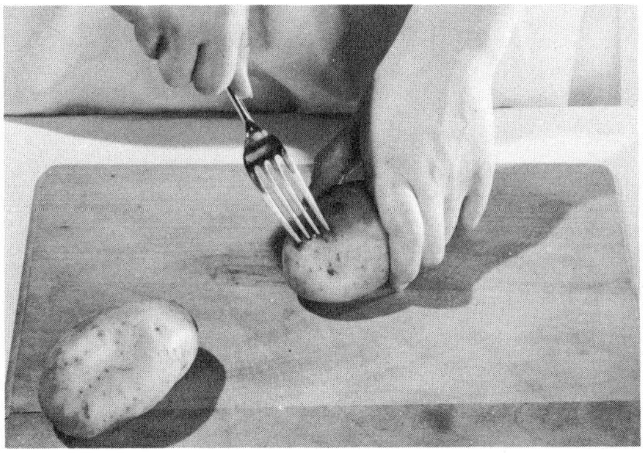
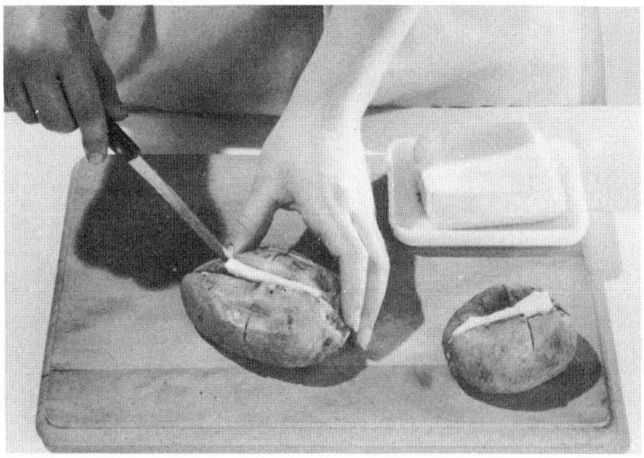
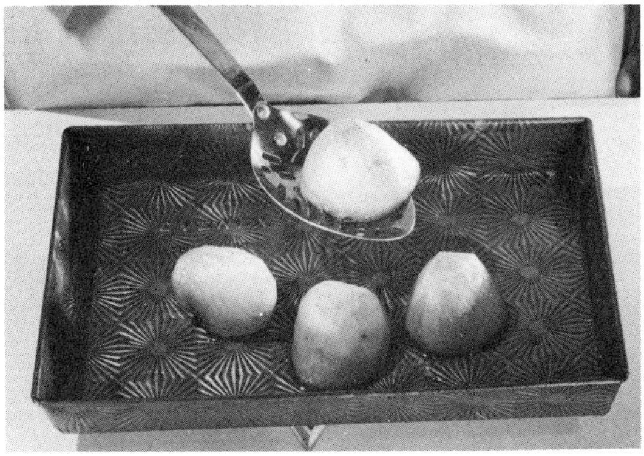
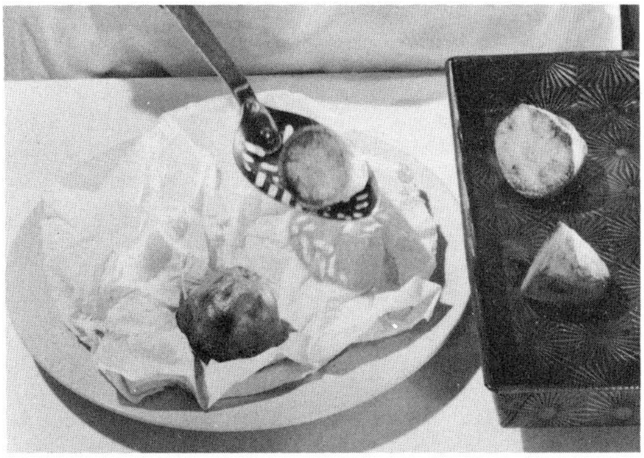
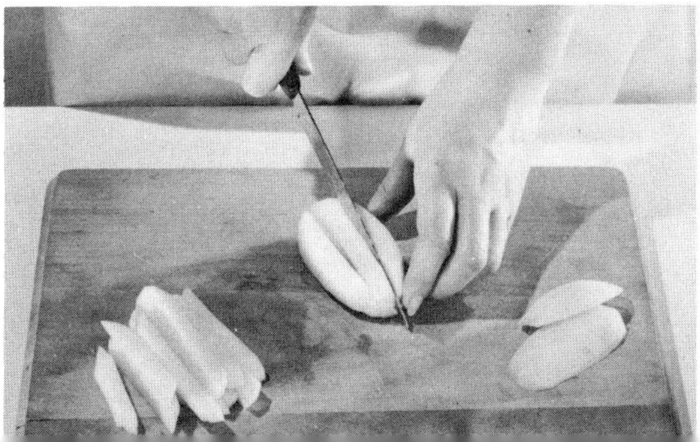
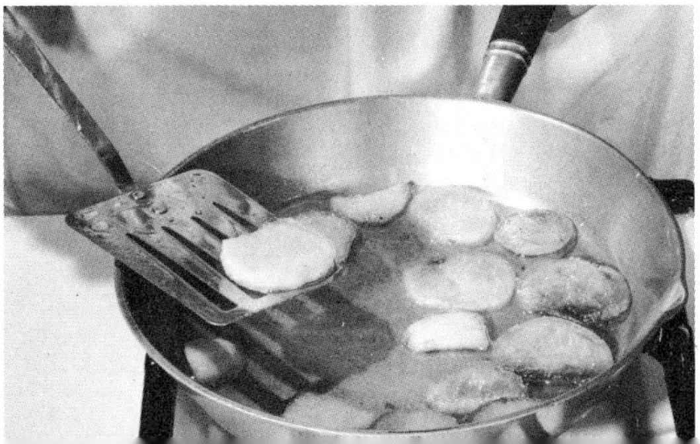

Vegetables

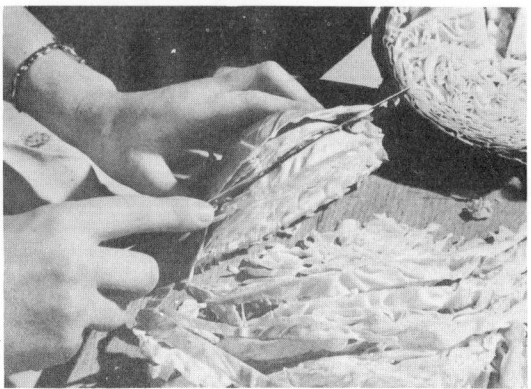

Cabbage: Remove outer leaves and hard stalk, then shred leaves

CABBAGE

Remove the coarse outer leaves, cut the cabbage in half and cut out the hard centre stalk. Shred the leaves finely, wash, drain and cook rapidly in about 1 inch of boiling salted water for 10-15 minutes, or until just done. Drain well and toss with a knob of butter, a sprinkling of pepper and a pinch of nutmeg (optional). Serve at once.

SPRING GREENS

Separate the leaves and cut off the base of any thick stems. Wash well, then shred roughly. Cook as for cabbage, but allow only 8-10 minutes.

BRUSSELS SPROUTS

Remove the outer leaves, cut a cross in the bottom of the stems, wash, then cook rapidly in boiling salted water for about 15-20 minutes, or until just cooked. Drain well, then toss with a little butter and a sprinkling of pepper.

Brussels sprouts: remove outer leaves and cut a cross in the base

CAULIFLOWER

Remove any coarse outer leaves, but leave the small ones intact. Trim the base of the stem and cut a cross in it, then wash the cauliflower well. Cook, stem side down, in fast-boiling salted water for about 20-30 minutes, depending on size. Drain well and, if you like, serve coated with a white or cheese sauce.
The cauliflower can be divided into individual florets and cooked in fast-boiling water for about 15 minutes. Drain well and serve tossed with butter and a sprinkling of pepper or coated with a cheese sauce.

SPINACH

Remove the stalks and any damaged leaves and wash very thoroughly in several waters, to remove grit or mud. Pack it into a saucepan with only the water that clings to it, heat gently and cook until it is cooked—about 10-15 minutes. Drain thoroughly, then chop or sieve as required. Add a small knob of butter or margarine and some salt and pepper before serving.

VEGETABLE MARROW

Peel the marrow, remove the seeds and cut the flesh into large cubes. Cook in a little boiling salted water for 15-20 minutes, until soft; drain really well. Toss with butter and a sprinkling of pepper and chopped parsley or coat with a well-seasoned white sauce.

ONIONS

Cut off the roots and remove the thin, papery brown skin. (Use a fork to prevent the smell clinging to hands.) Cook in boiling salted water for 30-45 minutes (longer for large ones), drain well and serve with a white or cheese sauce.

LEEKS

Remove the coarse outer leaves and cut off the roots and green tops. Split the leaf end down so that the leeks can be thoroughly washed and any soil or grit removed. Cook in boiling salted water until just soft—about 30 minutes—then drain carefully. Leeks may be served plain on toast (which is not eaten, but absorbs any surplus liquid). They are more usually coated with a white sauce and are particularly good served in a cheese sauce and sprinkled with finely grated cheese.

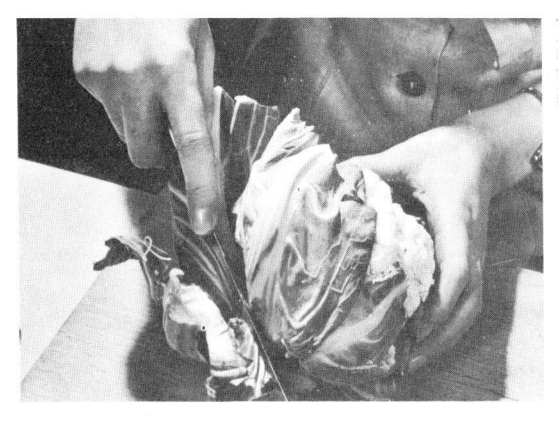

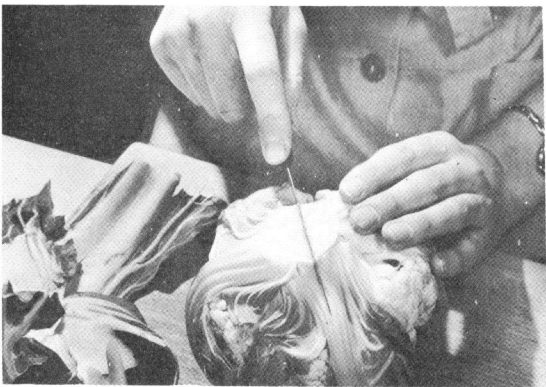

Cauliflower: Remove outer leaves and trim base of stem, then cut a cross in it

MUSHROOMS

Grilled—prepare the mushrooms, place on the grill rack, dot with butter, add a sprinkling of salt and pepper and cook under gentle heat for 5-10 minutes, until cooked.

Sautéed—prepare the mushrooms, leaving them whole or cutting in slices as preferred. Cook gently until soft in about 1 oz. butter with some salt and pepper, shake them from time to time. A squeeze of lemon juice can be added just before serving.

Baked—place the prepared whole mushrooms in a greased ovenproof dish, dot with butter, add a little salt and pepper, then cover with foil or greaseproof paper and bake in the centre of a moderate oven (350°F., mark 4) for about 15 minutes, or until cooked.

Onions: Use fork when peeling. Leeks: Trim, then split to make it easier to wash out all grit

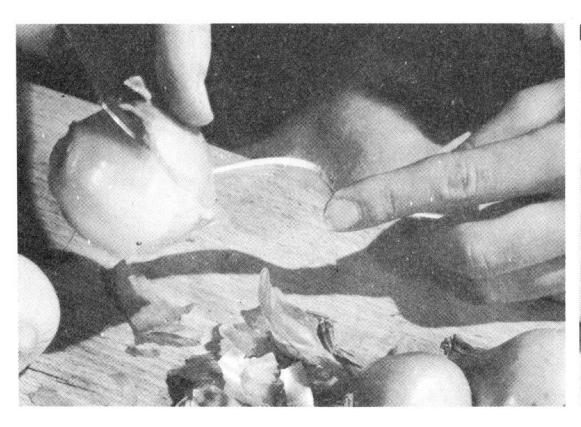

Vegetables

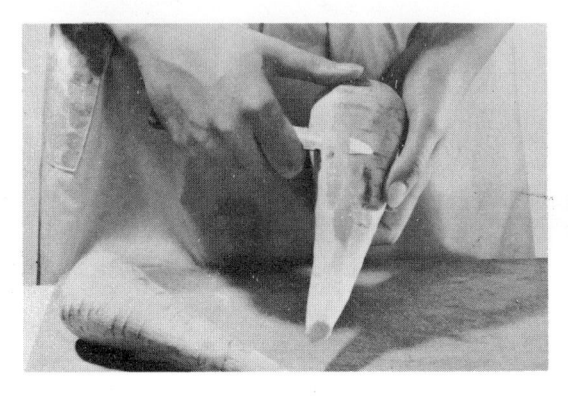

Peel parsnips thinly and cut into chunks; carrots may be cut into dice, slices or matchsticks

PARSNIPS

Peel these thinly and cut into quarters, or into even-sized pieces if large. They are very good cooked in the dripping round roast meat—allow about 1 hour. Otherwise, boil them in salted water until tender, allowing $\frac{1}{2}$-$\frac{3}{4}$ hour, according to their age and size. Drain and toss with a knob of butter or margarine and some chopped parsley. Alternatively, mash the parsnips well with butter and pepper.

TURNIPS

Peel rather thickly, cut either in pieces or dice and cook in salted water until tender; the time will vary considerably, from 20 minutes to $\frac{3}{4}$ hour, according to their age and whether the pieces are large or small. Drain and add pepper and a little butter or margarine; they may also be mashed.

SWEDES

These are prepared and cooked like turnips. They are sometimes diced and cooked with diced turnips or carrots.

Peel turnips thickly. Beetroots are not peeled until after they have been cooked

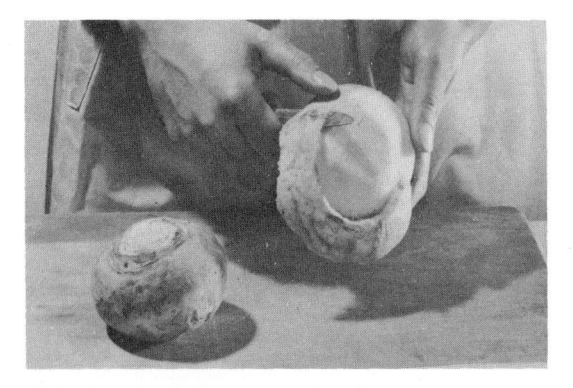

CARROTS

New—Trim off the leaves, then scrape lightly with a sharp knife. Small new carrots are usually cooked whole. Simmer in salted water for about 15 minutes or until cooked and serve tossed with a little butter, pepper and chopped parsley.

Old—peel thinly and cut into $\frac{1}{4}$-$\frac{1}{2}$ inch lengthways strips; these strips can then be cut across into small squares (dice). Alternatively, cut them into thin rounds. Simmer in salted water until tender—20-40 minutes depending on the method of cutting and the age of the carrots. Serve as for new carrots, or in a cheese sauce.

BEETROOTS

Cut off the leaves, leaving 1 inch of stem and taking care not to damage the skins. Wash the beetroots and boil them in salted water until tender—about 2 hours. Peel off the skin, cut off the stems and roots and cut the beetroot into cubes or slices; serve hot, coated with a white sauce. (See also Salad Ingredients, page 66).

GREEN PEAS

Shell the peas and place in boiling salted water with 1 level tsp. sugar and a sprig of fresh mint. Boil till cooked—about 20 minutes; drain, take out the mint and add a small knob of butter or margarine.

Salad: P. 66

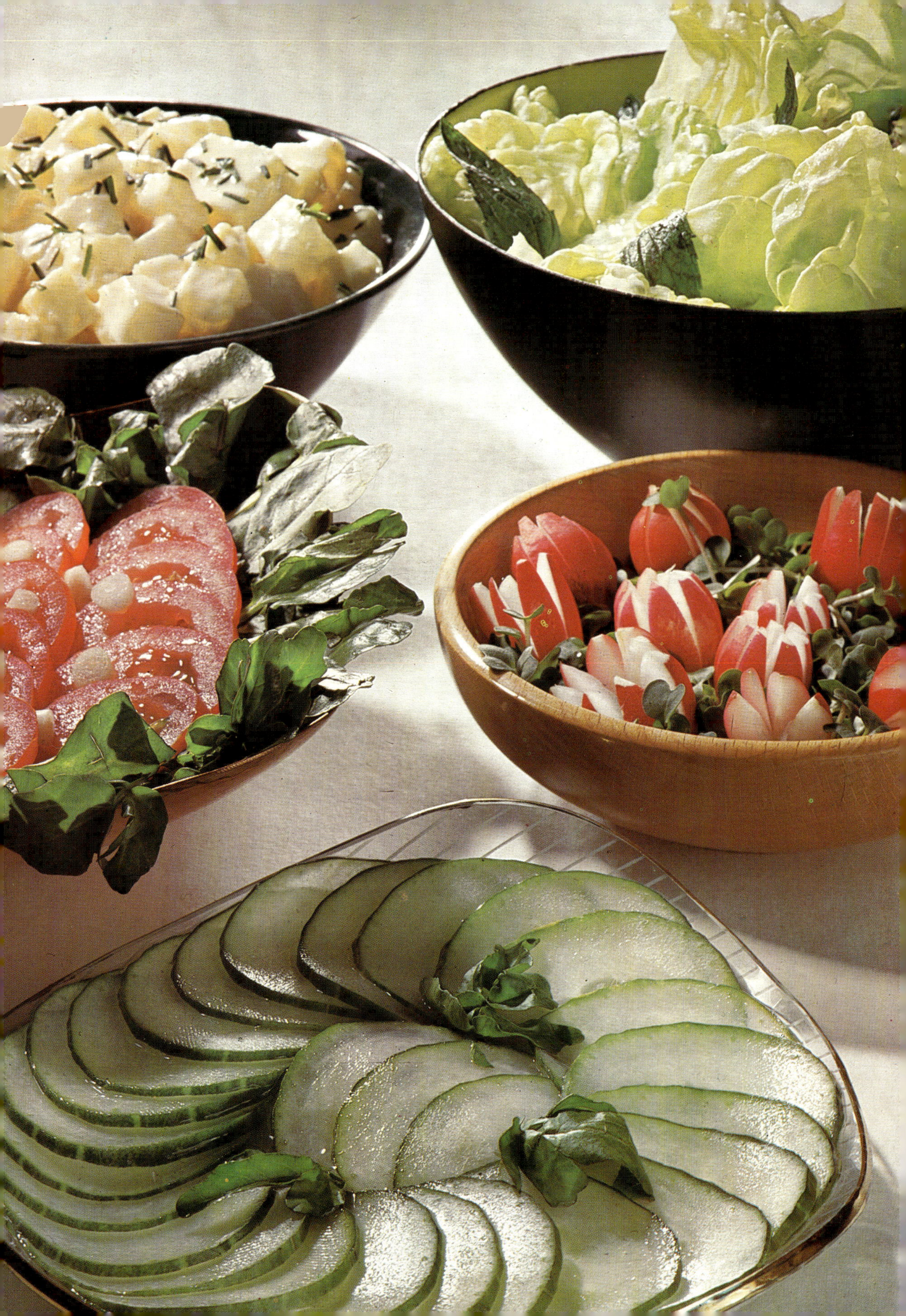

Edam
Cheddar
Wensleydale
Stilton
Port Salut
Red Cheshire
Camembert

BROAD BEANS

Shell the beans, cook them in boiling salted water for 20-30 minutes until tender and drain. Serve with parsley sauce or tossed with a knob of butter and a little chopped parsley.

FRENCH AND RUNNER BEANS

French—top, tail and wash the beans. Cook whole in boiling salted water for 10-15 minutes.

Runner—top, tail and cut diagonally into ½-inch slices. Cook in boiling salted water for about 20 minutes, until tender.

French and runner beans should be served tossed in butter with a sprinkling of pepper.

CORN ON THE COB

Remove the sheath and silky threads from the corn. Cook in boiling water for 12-20 minutes, or until the kernels are soft. Serve with melted butter; put a cocktail stick in each end of the cobs to make them easier to eat.

CELERY

Wash celery thoroughly, using a brush to remove all soil from the grooves of the outer stalks. Cut the stalks in even lengths and cook in boiling salted water until soft—½-¾ hour, according to the coarseness of the celery. Drain carefully and serve coated with a white or cheese sauce.

French beans are merely topped and tailed; Celery needs scrubbing before it is cut up

Braised Celery Hearts

Celery hearts Salt and pepper
Butter Stock from a cube

The inner parts of the celery are generally used for this dish, but the outer stalks may also be cut up and cooked in this way. Fry the celery in a little hot butter till very lightly browned. Season, then half-cover with stock. Cook gently with the lid on the pan until soft, or bake in a warm oven (325°F., mark 3) for ¾-1 hour.

TOMATOES

Grilled—choose even-sized tomatoes; halve and place on the grid, cut side uppermost. Put a small piece of butter and a sprinkling of pepper on each and cook under medium heat for 5-10 minutes, depending on their size.

Baked—prepare as for grilled tomatoes and place in a greased ovenproof dish. Add butter and pepper, cover with foil or greaseproof paper and bake in the centre of a moderate oven (350°F., mark 4) for about 15 minutes.

Corn on the cob is easier to handle if mounted on cocktail sticks; Tomatoes for grilling need to be seasoned and dotted with butter

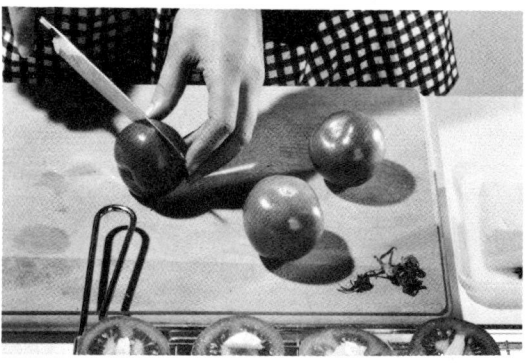

Favourite Cheeses: P. 72

Salads

Preparing Salad Ingredients

Lettuce—separate the leaves and wash them under a running cold tap or in a bowl of cold water. Drain the lettuce by shaking it in a clean tea-towel or in a salad basket or colander.

Watercress—trim the coarse ends from the stalks and place the watercress in a bowl of cold water, adding 2 level tsps. salt. Drain well.

Mustard and Cress—trim off the roots and lower part of the stems with scissors and place the leaves in a colander or sieve. Wash (under a fast-running cold tap, if possible), turning the cress over to remove any seeds.

Herbs (e.g. parsley or mint)—remove any large stems, wash the leaves in a colander or sieve, shake and allow to drain well, then chop with a cook's knife.

Spring Onions—trim off the root end with a vegetable knife, remove the outer papery skin and trim the green leaves down to about 2 inches.

Radishes—trim off the root end and leaves, place the radishes in cold water and rub well to remove any dirt. Leave whole, if small; if large, slice thinly into rings or make into flowers. (See also colour picture facing page 64.)

Simple Radish Flowers—make 6-8 small, deep cuts, crossing in the centre, at the stem end of the radish. Leave in cold water for 1-2 hours, until the cut parts open out to form petals.

Tomatoes—if these are to be peeled, dip them in a pan of boiling water for a minute, then place in a basin of cold water—the skin should then peel off easily. Slice thinly or cut into 6-8 segments, or treat as below.

Tomato Water-Lilies—make V-shaped cuts all round the middle of a tomato, taking the cuts right to the centre; then carefully pull the two halves apart.

Celery—separate the sticks and scrub well in cold water to remove any dirt. Slice, chop or make into "curls", as follows.

Celery Curls—cut into strips about $\frac{1}{4}$ inch wide and 2 inches long. Make cuts along the length of each strip, close together and to within $\frac{1}{2}$ inch of one end. Leave the pieces in cold water for 1-2 hours, until the strips curl.

Cucumber—wipe and cut into very thin slices. To give a deckled effect as shown, cut thin strips from the skin with a sharp knife before slicing the cucumber. If you like, place the cucumber slices in a small dish and cover with distilled or white vinegar. (See colour picture facing page 64.) To make a cucumber cone, make a cut from centre to rim of a slice, then wrap one cut edge over the other to make a funnel shape.

Cabbage—wash a few leaves in cold water and soak for about 15 minutes in water (adding 2 level tsps. salt if there is any sign of greenfly on the leaves.) Drain well, then chop finely with a cook's knife or grate, using the large holes on the grater.

Carrot—peel and cut into thin rings if new, or grate (using the large holes of the grater) if old.

Beetroot—these can be bought ready cooked. Peel thinly, then cut into dice or grate. Put in a small dish, sprinkle with salt and pepper and cover with vinegar.

Eggs—hard-boil, shell and cut in slices or quarters.

The pictures opposite show, from top to bottom: Washing and draining lettuce; Preparing watercress; Chopping parsley and mint; Trimming spring onions; Halving tomatoes; Making radish "flowers"; Making cucumber cones

67

Salads

Salad Dressings

French Salad Dressing: Measuring out the dry ingredients, adding the vinegar; Mixing the dressing

French Salad Dressing

½ level tsp. salt   A pinch of sugar
¼ tsp. pepper   1 tbsp. vinegar
½ level tsp. mustard   2 tbsps. olive oil

Put the salt, pepper, mustard and sugar together in a basin, add the vinegar and mix well, then blend in the olive oil, using a fork.

This is the dressing most commonly used for green salads (see colour picture facing page 64) and for simple mixed salads. It may be varied in several ways—for example:

With Parsley or other Herbs or Flavourings—make French dressing in the usual way and add some freshly chopped parsley, mint or other fresh herbs. Chopped gherkins, pickles or capers can also be included in the dressing, to add interest and flavour.

With Chopped Olives—chop a few stuffed olives and add to French dressing made as above.

Salad Creams

For speed and convenience most people tend to buy their salad cream ready made and bottled, but even so you need not serve it just as it is—it can be flavoured or "dressed up" as follows (in each case, start with ¼ pint salad cream.)

With Herbs (e.g., parsley, mint, chives)—chop enough herbs to produce 1 level tbsp. and add, with a squeeze of lemon juice.

With Lemon or Orange—grate the rind from a lemon or orange and squeeze out the juice. Stir the rind and sufficient juice to taste into the salad cream.

Piquant Dressing—chop some gherkins and capers and add 2 tsps. of each to the salad cream. A little of the vinegar from the gherkins or capers can also be added.

Tomato Dressing—add ½-1 tbsp. tomato ketchup or 1-2 tsps. tomato purée to the cream; 1-2 tbsps. cream or top of the milk improves this dressing.

Horseradish Dressing—add 1 level tbsp. horseradish cream and a squeeze of lemon juice.

Cream Dressing—a real transformation can be made by adding ⅛-¼ pint whipped cream.

Curry Dressing—blend 2-3 level tsps. curry powder with a little cream or top of the milk and stir into the salad cream.

Cheese Dressing—blend 2 oz. cream cheese with a little cream or top of the milk and stir into the salad cream. A little chopped chives or grated onion could also be added.

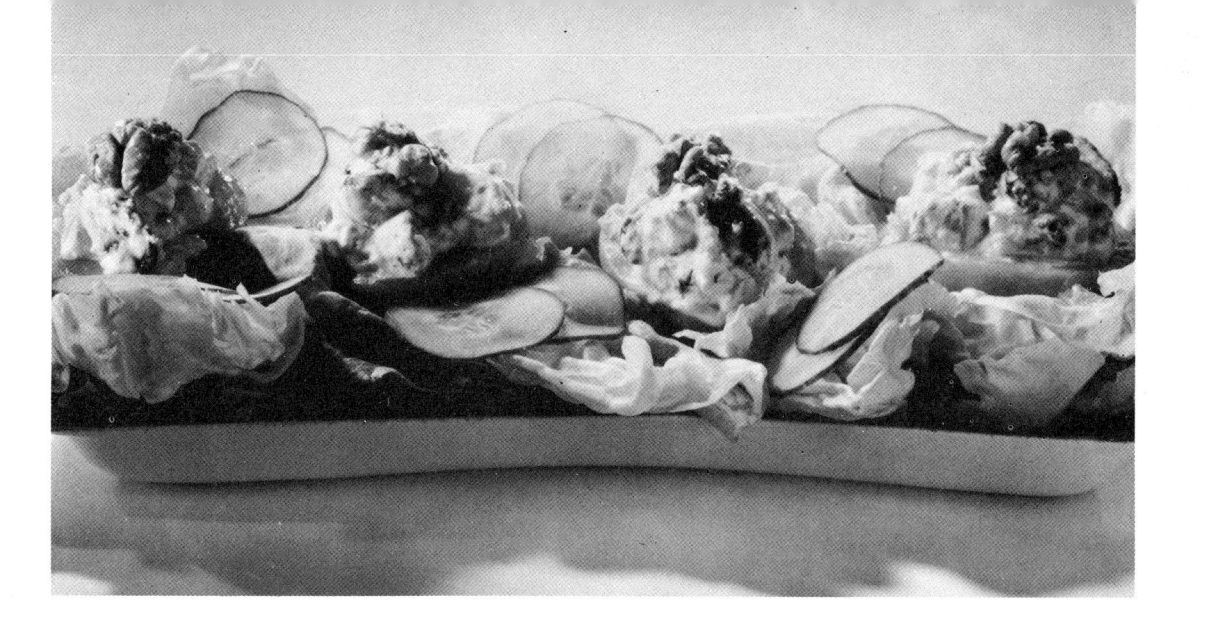

Cole Slaw

¼ of a hard white cabbage
½ a green pepper
2-3 sticks of celery
1 red-skinned eating apple
Salad cream

Shred the cabbage finely, cut the pepper into thin strips, chop the celery and dice the apple or cut in segments. Mix all these ingredients together and bind with salad cream. Serve garnished with a few strips of green pepper and segments of apple.
Note: 1-2 oz. crushed walnuts can be included.

Above: Peach and Cream Cheese Salad;
Below: Cole Slaw

Peach and Cream Cheese Salad

8 oz. curd cheese
1 tbsp. raisins
Lettuce
4 tinned peach halves
4 walnut halves
Cucumber or watercress to garnish

Beat the cheese until smooth. Put the raisins into boiling water for 1-2 minutes to soften them, drain well and cool, then mix with the cheese. Put the lettuce on a dish in about 4 individual portions and place in each one of the peach halves (or 2-3 apricot halves). Top each with 1 tbsp. of the cheese-and-raisin mixture and decorate with a walnut half. Garnish the dish with cucumber or watercress.

Salads

Tomato Salad

4 tomatoes
A little chopped onion
Salt and pepper
2 tbsps. salad oil
1 tbsp. vinegar
Chopped parsley (optional)

Skin the tomatoes and slice them fairly thinly. Arrange in a dish, sprinkle with chopped onion and seasoning and add the mixed oil and vinegar. Sprinkle with parsley. (See also colour picture facing page 64.)

Potato Salad

½ lb. cooked potatoes
2–3 spring onions
Salad cream
Finely chopped parsley or chives
Watercress (optional)

Dice the potatoes and slice the spring onions. Mix both with salad cream, pile into a dish, sprinkle with parsley or chives and garnish, if liked, with watercress. (See also colour picture facing page 64.)

Orange Salad

Peel 2 oranges and cut into sections, removing all skin and pith, or cut them across thinly, using a saw-edged knife. Put into a shallow dish and sprinkle with a little chopped tarragon and chervil, if available; otherwise use a little chopped mint. Blend 1 tbsp. oil, 2 tsps. vinegar and 1 tsp. lemon juice, pour over the fruit and allow to stand for a short time before serving. The orange slices can be laid on a bed of watercress, cress or lettuce, before the dressing is poured over them.

Egg Salad

Slice 3 hard-boiled eggs and arrange them in overlapping rings in the opposite quarters of a round plate. Put 2 sliced tomatoes in one of the empty quarters and some potato salad in the other. Sprinkle with finely chopped parsley and chopped celery (or spring onion) and garnish with small cress.

Winter Salad 1

Cooked peas (frozen or canned)
Cooked carrots, diced
Potato salad
Shredded cooked beetroot
Shredded cabbage
Chopped parsley

Arrange the separate ingredients in lines on a large platter and sprinkle with parsley. Any colourful assortment of raw or cooked vegetables that are available can be used for a winter salad.

Winter Salad 2

3–4 sticks celery
1 cooked beetroot
1 eating apple
½ a small onion
Salad cream

Wash and chop the celery; peel and dice the beetroot; quarter, core and dice the apple; grate or finely chop the onion. Mix these ingredients together and add just enough salad cream to bind.

Below: Tomato Salad

Potato Salad

Egg Salad

Winter Salad

Cheese
and Cheese Cookery

Cheese is one of the things that are best bought in fairly small quantities, once or twice a week, since many types do not keep particularly well.

Store it in a cool place, loosely covered with greaseproof paper or a polythene bag, or in a cheese dish with a ventilated cover. Do not make it airtight, or the cheese will tend to go mouldy—on the other hand, if it is not covered at all, cheese becomes hard and dry. If several types are being stored, wrap each separately, so that the flavours do not blend.

If you keep it in the refrigerator, it is better to remove it ½–1 hour before serving, so that its full flavour can be restored.

TYPES OF ENGLISH CHEESE

Caerphilly—white cheese with a crumbly texture and mild flavour; best eaten uncooked.

Cheddar—hard, yellow, slightly salty cheese, varying in flavour from mild to quite strong. It is very good for cooking, but is also a popular table cheese.

Cheshire—can be obtained in two forms—white or red (actually a creamy-orange colour). It is a mild, crumbly cheese, equally good for cooking or for table use.

Gloucester—orange-yellow, hard cheese with a close, crumbly texture and a flavour similar to that of Cheshire. It is not often used in cooking.

Lancashire—a white, fairly hard cheese, crumbly in texture when cut. It has a flavour which varies from mild to quite strong when the cheese becomes mature. It is an excellent cooking cheese, but is equally good served uncooked.

Stilton—fairly hard, white cheese with blue veins running through it and a characteristic grey crinkly rind. It has an excellent flavour and is one of the best-known English cheeses. It is not used in cooking.

Wensleydale—white, crumbly cheese with a mild flavour. It is usually served as it is, but can be used for cooking.

POPULAR CONTINENTAL CHEESES

Unless otherwise stated, these are usually eaten as bought and not used in cooking.

Bel Paese—a creamy, mild cheese made in Italy.

Brie—a flat, round mild-flavoured French cheese, with a brown, slightly mouldy crust. It should be bought in small amounts, as it does not keep well.

Camembert—a small, round cheese, soft and creamy in texture usually sold boxed. It should not be allowed to get too ripe, as it develops an unpleasant smell and taste.

Danish Blue—a crumbly white cheese with blue veining. It has a sharp, salty taste.

Edam—a Dutch cheese, ball-shaped and with a red skin. It is yellow in colour, firm in texture and mild-flavoured.

Gorgonzola—a fairly firm, blue-veined cheese with a sharp flavour, made in Italy.

Gruyerè—a firm yellow cheese, originally Swiss made, with a smooth texture broken by "eyes" or "holes". It has a distinctive rather sour flavour. It can be used in cooking or eaten as it is. Also produced as processed foil-wrapped portions.

Parmesan—a very hard Italian cheese with a black outer crust and a rough texture. It can be bought in the piece, but is more conveniently bought ready grated in small packs, as it is used mainly in cooking.

Port Salut—a French cheese with a creamy yellow colour, fairly soft texture and mild flavour.

The Cheese Course

A cheese board or platter makes a simple but enjoyable way of finishing a meal and is equally popular as a snack to offer when friends drop in or as a buffet party

dish. To produce a really attractive effect:
1. Use a flat board or platter for easy cutting.
2. Aim at variety in colour, texture and shape in the cheeses. You should have at least three types—white, yellow or blue, flat, round, wedge-shaped or in individual portions, hard or creamy. (See colour picture facing page 65.)
3. Have the bread (French, wholemeal, rye) cut in chunks for speedy serving. Have also some biscuits, plain, savoury or semi-sweet, and perhaps crispbread.
4. Butter can be served in a block or ready-cut into cubes.
5. Any of the following can be served with cheese: Salad ingredients such as lettuce, chicory, celery, carrot sticks, radishes, tomatoes, spring onions and watercress, or fresh fruit in season.

Cheese on Toast

¼ lb. Cheddar, Lancashire, or Cheshire cheese
2 thick slices of bread
Butter
Salt and pepper
¼ level tsp. dry mustard (or a few drops of Worcestershire sauce)
A little milk to mix
2 tomatoes, halved

Grate the cheese. Toast and butter the bread and keep warm. Mix the cheese and seasonings with enough milk to make a spreadable mixture. Pile on to the toast, taking it right up to the edges. Cook under a hot grill until golden and bubbly and grill the tomatoes at the same time. Serve as shown.

Cheese on Toast: Mixing and spreading the cheese topping and serving the grilled toasts

Cheese and cheese cookery

Macaroni Cheese

Salt, pepper and mustard
4-6 oz. macaroni
1½ oz. margarine
1½ oz. flour
1 pint milk
6 oz. cheese, grated
1 tomato, sliced

Grease an ovenproof dish. Half-fill a large saucepan with water, bring to the boil and add 2 level tsps. salt. Drop in the macaroni (breaking it up if necessary) and cook rapidy till soft—about 20 minutes for "regular" type, 5 minutes for "quick" kind. Make a white sauce (see Roux Sauce, page 87) with the margarine, flour and milk and add the cheese, saving 2-3 tbsps. for the topping. Season to taste with salt, pepper and mustard.

Drain the cooked macaroni, add to the cheese sauce and mix thoroughly. Put into the dish and sprinkle with the remaining cheese. Arrange the tomato on the top and put under a hot grill until the cheese is golden.

Adding the drained cooked macaroni to the sauce and topping with cheese after transferring to a dish

Cheese and Vegetable Flan

4 oz. plain flour
½ level tsp. salt
1 oz. lard
2 oz. margarine
Water to mix

1 small pkt. frozen mixed vegetables
1 oz. flour
½ pint milk
4 oz. cheese, grated
Salt and pepper

Make some shortcrust pastry (see page 92) with the flour, salt, lard, 1 oz. margarine and water to mix. Use to line a 7-inch flan case and bake blind (see page 96). Cook the frozen vegetables. Meanwhile, make a white roux sauce (see page 87) with the remaining margarine, the flour and the milk. Add three-quarters of the cheese, then the drained cooked vegetables; mix well and season to taste. Pour into the flan case, sprinkle with the rest of the cheese and put under a hot grill until the cheese is golden-brown.

Combining the cooked vegetables with the sauce and filling the flan case

Cheese and cheese cookery

Cheese Pudding

5-6 slices of bread and butter
2 eggs
A little made mustard
Salt and pepper
2 tsps. Worcestershire sauce
1 pint milk
4 oz. cheese, grated
1 oz. breadcrumbs

Heat the oven to moderate (350°F., mark 4). Cut the bread and butter into squares and arrange neatly in a greased ovenproof dish. Beat the eggs and add the seasonings, sauce, milk and three-quarters of the cheese. Pour this mixture over the bread and butter and allow to stand for 15 minutes. Sprinkle with the rest of the cheese and breadcrumbs and bake in the centre of the oven for 45 minutes, until well risen and golden-brown.

Putting the bread and butter in the dish;
mixing the egg and cheese sauce;
pouring it into the dish;
topping with cheese and breadcrumbs

Cheese and Onion Pie

6 oz. plain flour
½ level tsp. salt
1½ oz. lard
1½ oz. margarine
Water to mix
2 large onions
Salt and pepper
1 egg
8 oz. Cheddar cheese, grated
A little milk

Heat the oven to fairly hot (400°F., mark 6). Make some shortcrust pastry from the flour, salt, lard, margarine and water (see page 92). Chop the onions and cook in a little salted water until soft—about 10 minutes—then drain them. Beat the egg in a medium-sized basin and add to the cheese and onion; season with salt and pepper. Halve the pastry and roll out one piece thinly on a floured board into a round a little bigger than a 7-inch pie plate. Line the plate with the pastry, taking care not to stretch it. Fill the centre with the cheese and onion mixture. Roll out the remaining pastry to fit the top of the dish and put in place, damping the edges of the pastry before pressing them together. Hold down the edge of the pastry with the back of the first finger and make close horizontal cuts round the edge. Now, using the back of the knife blade, "pull up" the edge of the pastry at 1-inch intervals to form scallops. Brush the top of the pie with milk. Put the pie on a baking tray and cook near the top of the oven for about 30 minutes, until the pastry is golden.

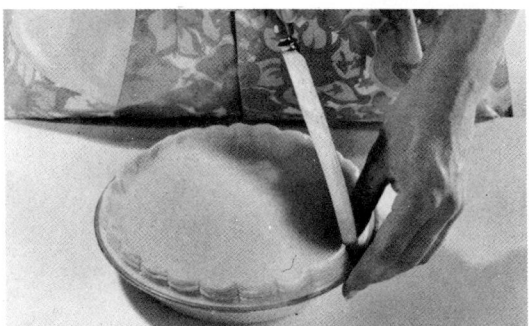

*Chopping the onions;
mixing the filling;
putting it into the pastry case;
decorating the edges*

Cheese and cheese cookery

Oven Omelette

4 oz. bacon, chopped
½ an onion, chopped
1 level tbsp. chopped parsley
2 level tsps. flour

4 eggs
¼ pint milk
Salt and pepper
4 oz. cheese, grated

Heat the oven to moderate (350°F., mark 4). Fry the bacon until crisp, then drain, leaving the fat in the pan, and put the bacon into a deep pie plate. Add the onion and parsley to the fat and fry until soft. Add the flour, stir well and then add to the bacon. Beat the eggs with the milk and seasoning and pour into the pie plate. Sprinkle with the cheese and bake in the oven for 30 minutes, or until set and golden-brown.

Removing the cooked bacon from the pan; adding the flour to the fried onion and parsley; pouring the omelette mixture into the dish; sprinkling with cheese

Ham and Leeks au Gratin

4 large or 8 small leeks
Salt and pepper
1 oz. butter
1 oz. flour
½ pint leek liquor, made up with milk
3 oz. Cheddar cheese, grated
4-8 slices of cooked ham

Prepare the leeks by trimming the leaves and cutting off the roots; split then wash thoroughly under running water. Cook for about 20 minutes in boiling salted water; when done, drain well. Melt the butter, add the flour to make a roux and gradually add the leek liquor and milk. Bring to the boil and cook for 2-3 minutes; remove from the heat and add two-thirds of the grated cheese. Heat the grill. Wrap a slice of ham round each leek and place in an ovenproof dish, pour the cheese sauce over and sprinkle the remaining grated cheese on top. Brown lightly under the grill.

*Making a sauce with the liquor;
rolling the leeks in ham;
pouring the sauce over;
topping with cheese*

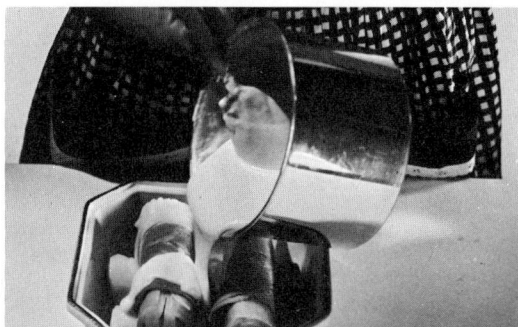

Rice and Pasta

Boiled Rice—Classic method

Allow 1½-2 oz. long-grain rice per person. Put a large pan of salted water on to boil. When it comes to the boil, add the rice; as soon as the water returns to the boil stir well, then boil (uncovered) for 15-20 minutes, until the grains are just soft. Turn the rice into a sieve and pour boiling water through it to separate the grains. Grease a piece of greaseproof paper and place it on a baking tray. Spread the rice out on the paper, cover lightly and place in a cool oven (325°F., mark 3) for about 10 minutes, to dry out.

The "1-2-1" method for Boiled Rice

Put into a saucepan 1 cup of long-grain rice, 2 cups water, 1 level tsp. salt and a squeeze of lemon juice (optional). Bring to the boil, stir and cover with a lid. Reduce the heat and simmer for 14-15 minutes, until all the liquid has been absorbed and the grains are just soft.
Note: Rice cooked by this method does not require rinsing with hot water and draining.

Boiled Spaghetti

Allow 1-1½ oz. spaghetti per person. Heat a large pan of salted water; when it comes to the boil, place the ends of the long strands of spaghetti in the pan and hold there until pliable, then coil them round in the pan. Boil for 15-20 minutes, until just soft, turn the spaghetti into a sieve and drain. Return it to the saucepan with a knob of butter and heat gently, so that the butter coats the spaghetti.

Noodles

Cook as for spaghetti.

From top to bottom; rinsing boiled rice and spreading it out to dry; putting spaghetti into boiling water and draining it

Spaghetti Bolognese: P. 83

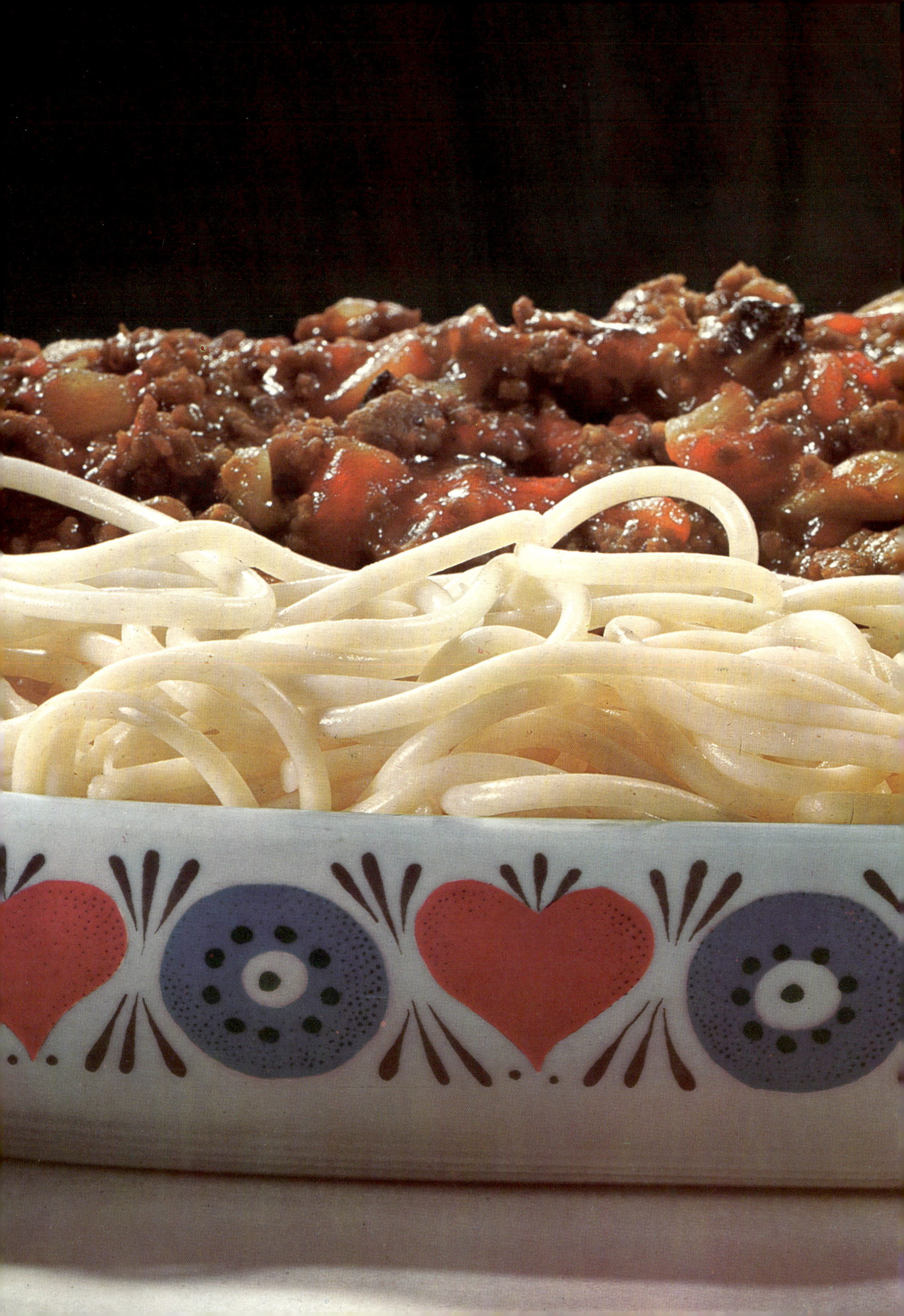

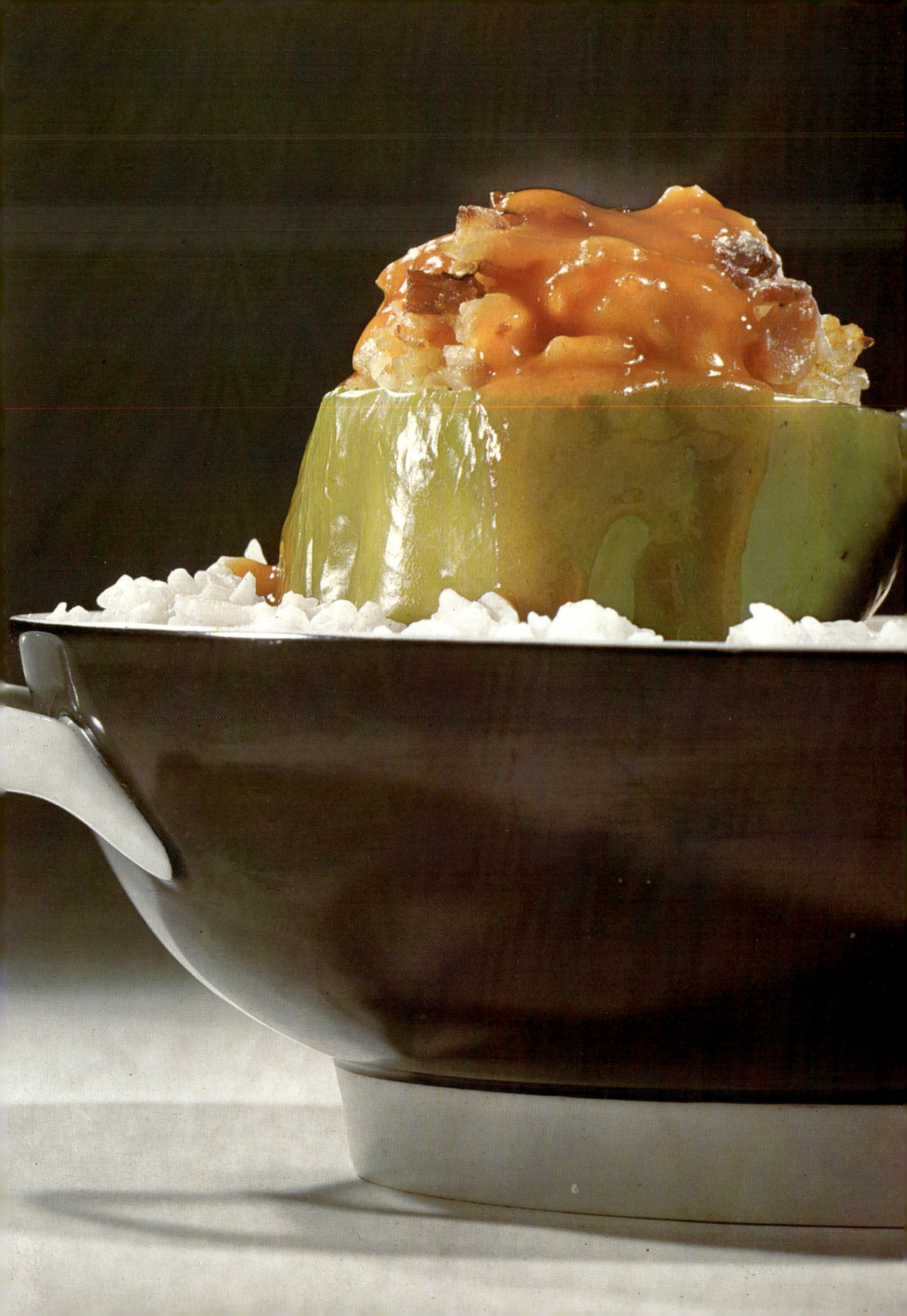

Stuffed Green Peppers

4 green peppers
1½ oz. butter
1 onion, chopped
4 tomatoes, skinned and chopped
4 oz. bacon, chopped
4 oz. boiled rice
Salt and pepper
2 oz. Cheddar cheese, grated
1 oz. fresh breadcrumbs
¼ pint stock

Heat the oven to fairly hot (375°F., mark 5). Wipe the peppers and cut off the ends ½ inch below the stalk. Scoop out the seeds and core with a knife, then wash out the cases and stand them up in an ovenproof dish. Heat 1 oz. butter and lightly fry the onion and tomatoes; add the bacon and fry lightly. Add the cooked rice and seasoning and half the grated cheese. Mix the rest of the cheese with the breadcrumbs. Put the rice stuffing into the pepper cases and sprinkle with the breadcrumb mixture. Pour the stock round the base of the cases and cook just above the centre of the oven for 15-20 minutes, or until the pepper cases are cooked. Serve with rice or other accompaniment—see colour picture opposite.

*Scooping out the cores from the peppers;
making the filling;
stuffing the peppers;
topping with cheese and breadcrumbs*

Stuffed Green Peppers: opposite

Rice and Pasta

Noodles with Tomato Sauce

8 oz. noodles
2 tbsps. oil
2 cloves of garlic, peeled and chopped
1 15 oz. can of tomatoes
A bayleaf
1 level tsp. sugar
Salt and pepper
2 oz. grated Parmesan cheese (optional)

Heat a large pan of salted water; when it boils, add the noodles and cook for 15-20 minutes. Heat the oil in a shallow pan and gently fry the chopped garlic. Add the tomatoes, bayleaf, sugar and seasonings and simmer gently for 8-10 minutes. When the noodles are cooked, drain and arrange in a serving dish. Remove the bayleaf from the tomato sauce and pour the sauce over the noodles. Serve the cheese separately.

The canned tomatoes may be replaced by 1½ lb. fresh ones, skinned and chopped.

Cooking the noodles;
frying garlic;
adding the canned tomatoes;
pouring the sauce over the noodles

Spaghetti Bolognese

2 tbsps. oil
1 medium-sized onion, chopped
1 carrot, sliced
2 oz. bacon, chopped
1 lb. minced beef
1 8 oz. can of tomatoes
2 oz. mushrooms, sliced
Salt and pepper
A good dash of Worcestershire sauce
2 level tsps. sugar
2 tbsps. white wine or beer
6 oz. spaghetti

Put a large pan of salted water on to boil. Heat the oil in a large frying pan and lightly fry the onion, carrot and bacon. Add the minced beef and fry until well browned. Add the tomatoes and mushrooms, then the seasonings and wine, and simmer for 15-20 minutes. Wind the spaghetti into the pan of boiling water and boil for 15-20 minutes. When the spaghetti is cooked, drain and arrange on a dish. Pour the meat sauce into the centre of the dish—see colour picture facing page 80.

Note: The canned tomatoes may be replaced by ¾ lb. fresh tomatoes, skinned and chopped, or 2 tbsps. tomato paste.

Frying the ingredients for the meat sauce; adding the wine; cooking the spaghetti; adding the sauce to the spaghetti

Soups

Mixed Vegetable Soup

1 onion
2 potatoes
1 carrot
¼ of a head of celery
2 tomatoes, peeled
A bouquet garni
1 oz. butter
Salt and pepper
2 pints stock
3 level tbsps. flour
A little milk

Prepare the vegetables according to type and cut into neat, even-sized pieces. Make a bouquet garni of parsley stalks, a bay leaf, a pinch of mixed herbs, a clove and 2 peppercorns, tied in muslin. Melt the butter in the pan and fry the onion, then add all the other vegetables and put the lid on the pan. Sauté the vegetables for a few minutes, shaking the pan well until the fat is absorbed. Add the seasoning, stock and bouquet garni and simmer about 30 minutes until the vegetables are soft but not mushy. Blend the flour with a little cold milk, pour some of the hot liquid on to it, then stir the mixture into the saucepan. Bring to the boil, stirring all the time.

Mixed Vegetable Soup:
Preparing the vegetables and bouquet garni,
sautéing the vegetables and
adding the thickening

Potato Soup

1 oz. butter
2 lb. potatoes, peeled and sliced
1 onion, chopped
A stick of celery, chopped
2 pints stock
Salt and pepper
A bouquet garni
1 level tbsp. flour
¼ pint milk
1 tbsp. chopped parsley

Melt the butter and sauté the vegetables in it for 5–10 minutes. Add the stock, seasoning and bouquet garni, bring to the boil and simmer until the vegetables are soft and the potato breaks up—30 minutes. Remove the bouquet garni and mash the vegetables. Blend the flour with the milk and stir into the soup, bring to the boil and continue to boil for 2–3 minutes. Add the parsley just before serving.

French Onion Soup

1½ oz. butter
½ lb. onions, chopped
1 level tbsp. flour
1½ pints boiling stock
Salt and pepper
A bay leaf
Slices of French bread
Grated cheese

Melt the butter and fry the onions until they are well and evenly browned, taking care not to let the pieces become too dark. Add the flour and mix well. Pour on the boiling stock, add some salt and pepper and the bay leaf and simmer for 30 minutes; remove the bay leaf. Put the slices of French bread in a soup tureen, pour on the soup and top with grated cheese. Alternatively, pour the soup into a fireproof casserole, float the slices of bread on it and cover with the grated cheese; then brown under the grill for a few minutes.

Lentil Soup

1 oz. butter
4 oz. lentils, washed
¼ lb. carrots, sliced
¼ lb. onions, chopped
Stick of celery, chopped
A small piece of turnip, chopped
2 pints stock
Salt and pepper
A bouquet garni
1 level tbsp. cornflour
¼ pint milk
Chopped parsley to garnish

Melt the dripping and sauté the lentils and vegetables for about 10 minutes, stirring frequently to prevent sticking. Add the stock, seasoning and bouquet garni, bring to the boil, cover and allow to simmer gently until the lentils and vegetables are soft—1-1½ hours. Sieve the soup, return it to the pan and reheat. Blend the cornflour and milk and mix with the soup; add more seasoning if necessary. Bring to the boil, stirring all the time, and add the chopped parsley just before serving.

Celery Soup

1 oz. butter
1 medium head of celery, sliced
1 medium-sized onion, sliced
2 pints stock
Salt and pepper
A bouquet garni
3 level tbsps. flour
¼ pint milk
2-3 tbsps. cream
Parsley to garnish

Melt the butter and sauté the sliced celery and onion for 5-10 minutes. Add the stock, seasoning and bouquet garni, bring to the boil, stirring all the time, and simmer until the vegetables are quite soft—about 1-1½ hours. Sieve the soup and return it to the saucepan. Blend the flour with the milk, mix with the soup and allow to boil for a further 2-3 minutes. Re-season if necessary and add the cream and chopped parsley just before serving—don't heat again, or the cream may curdle.

Tomato Soup

1 oz. butter
1 stick of celery, chopped
1 small onion, finely chopped
1 carrot, sliced
1 rasher of bacon, chopped
2 level tbsps. flour
A bouquet garni
1½ lb. tomatoes, quartered
1 pint stock
Salt and pepper
A little sugar
Lemon juice

Melt the butter and cook the celery, onion, carrot and bacon for 5 minutes. Sprinkle in the flour and stir well. Add the bouquet garni, tomatoes, stock and seasoning. Cover and cook gently for 30 minutes. Sieve the soup, return it to the pan, check the seasoning, add a little sugar and lemon juice and reheat.

Tomato Soup:
Sautéing the flavouring vegetables and bacon, adding the flour, sieving, adding the sugar

Soups

Stock for Soups

A bouillon cube can be used as a basis—make it up as directed on the packet. Use a chicken cube for light-coloured soups (e.g., celery) and a beef cube for dark-coloured ones (e.g., kidney).

Soup Garnishes

Croûtons
Toast slices of bread and cut into neat dice just before serving. Suitable for almost all soups.

Grated Cheese
Grate Cheddar or Parmesan cheese and serve with potato, leek or onion soups.

Sausage
Slice cold cooked sausages (ordinary or smoked). Serve with celery, onion or pea soups.

Sour Cream
Whip the cream and chop some parsley. Spoon the cream on to tomato or kidney soup just before serving and sprinkle with chopped parsley.

Kidney Soup

1 oz. butter	1¾ pints stock
1 onion, chopped	Salt and pepper
2 sticks of celery, chopped	2 level tbsps. conflour
1 carrot, sliced	¼ pint stock or water to
½ lb. ox kidney, chopped	blend cornflour

Melt the butter, then sauté the vegetables for 5–10 minutes. Add the kidney, stock and seasonings, bring to the boil and simmer for 1½–2 hours. Sieve the soup. Blend the cornflour and stock, mix with the soup and bring to the boil, stirring all the time.

Chicken Soup

1 oz. cornflour	1 tsp. lemon juice
¼ pint milk	Ground nutmeg
2 pints chicken stock	Salt and pepper
4 oz. cooked chicken, diced	1 egg yolk
	2 tbsps. single cream

Blend the cornflour with a little of the milk. Boil the stock and pour it on to the blended mixture, stirring well. Return the mixture to the pan with the remaining milk and bring to the boil, stirring until the soup thickens. Cover and simmer gently for about 20 minutes. Add chicken, lemon juice, pinch of nutmeg and seasoning. Mix the egg yolk, and cream and add to the soup; reheat without boiling, until it thickens.

The stock may also be made by simmering a roast chicken carcase in water for 1–2 hours with a few pieces of onion and carrot and some herbs.

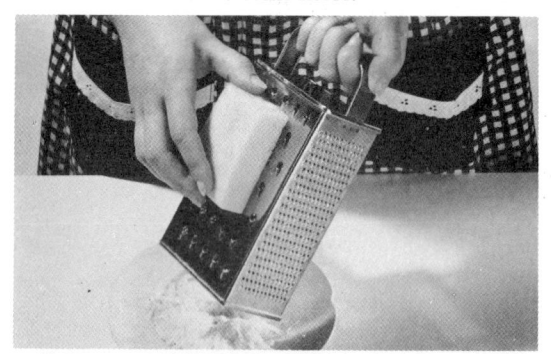

Garnishes: Croutons, grated cheese, sliced sausage, sour cream with parsley

Sauces
and Stuffings

White Roux Sauce (Basic Mixture)

1½ oz. butter or margarine
1½ oz. plain flour or cornflour
1 pint milk
Salt and pepper
Flavouring if required

Melt the fat in a small saucepan, add the flour or cornflour and stir well with a wooden spoon. Cook until the mixture bubbles, then remove it from the heat. Add the milk a little at a time, stirring thoroughly before adding any more. Return the sauce to the heat and bring to the boil, stirring all the time, until it thickens. Season to taste.

For a coating sauce use 2 oz. each of fat and flour to 1 pint milk.

This basic sauce can be infinitely varied by adding different flavourings—see this page.

White Roux Sauce: Mixing and cooking roux, adding liquid and boiling till thickened

VARIATIONS OF WHITE SAUCE

Use a basis of ½ pint white roux sauce.

Parsley—add 2 tbsps. chopped parsley. If the sauce is to accompany fish, add a little lemon juice or vinegar; stir thoroughly and reheat.

Cheese—to the hot sauce add 2–3 oz. grated cheese, a little mustard and a few drops of Worcestershire sauce.

Onion—chop 1–2 onions and cook in just enough water to cover until tender. Use ¼ pint cooking liquid and ¼ pint milk to make sauce, then add onion.

Egg—add 1–2 finely chopped hard-boiled eggs.

Anchovy—omit the salt. Add anchovy essence to taste (1–2 tbsps.) and a drop or two of pink colouring to tint.

Mushroom—add 2 oz. sliced sautéed button mushrooms and cook for 2–3 minutes.

Shrimp—add 1–2 oz. chopped shrimps (or prawns), with a little lemon juice and anchovy essence.

Caper—add 1–2 oz. capers (chopped or whole) and a little of the liquid or some lemon juice.

Tomato—add ½ lb. tomatoes, skinned and cut-up; simmer for about 5 minutes.

For Sweet Sauces, see page 131.

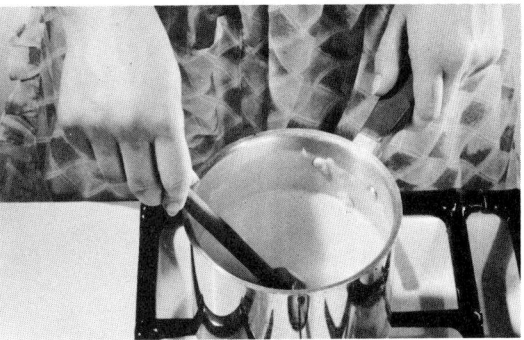

Sauces and Stuffings

White Blended Sauce

3 level tbsps. cornflour   Salt and pepper
1 pint milk   Flavouring (optional)

Put the cornflour into a bowl and mix to a thin paste with a little of the cold milk. Bring the rest of the milk to the boil, then pour onto the blended cornflour, stirring well bring to the boil. Return the mixture to the saucepan and stirring all the time, until the sauce thickens. Season to taste; this sauce may be varied like the roux sauce on the previous page.

Bread Sauce

A few cloves   3 oz. fresh breadcrumbs
1 onion $\frac{1}{2}$ oz. butter
$\frac{3}{4}$ pint milk   Salt and pepper

Stick the cloves into the onion, put in a saucepan with the milk and bring almost to the boil; leave for 20 minutes. Add the crumbs and butter and season to taste. Remove the onion and reheat.

Mint Sauce

Fresh mint   1 tbsp. boiling water
2 level tsps. sugar $1\frac{1}{2}$ tbsps. vinegar

Wash the mint and strip the leaves from the stalks; chop as finely as possible. Put the sugar into a sauceboat, pour on the boiling water, stir until dissolved, then add the chopped mint and vinegar.

When fresh mint is not obtainable, bottled mint may be used; in the case of a commercial preparation, follow the directions on the bottle.

Curry Sauce

1 oz. lard or butter   1 level tbsp. flour
2 level tbsps. chopped onion $\frac{1}{2}$ pint stock
   Salt
2 level tbsps. chopped apple   Lemon juice
   1 tbsp. chutney
2–4 level tsps. curry powder   1 tbsp. sultanas

Melt the fat in a pan and fry the onion lightly, then the apple and lastly the curry powder and flour. Stir in the stock gradually and add salt. Bring to the boil then add the remaining ingredients. Simmer with the lid on for about $\frac{1}{2}$ hour, stirring frequently. Use for curried fish, eggs and so on.

Gravy

A rich brown gravy is served with all roast joints. There should be no need to use extra colouring or flavouring if the gravy is properly made in the baking tin after the joint has been removed.

To make thin gravy, pour the fat very slowly from the tin, draining it off carefully from one corner and leaving the sediment behind. Season well with salt and pepper and add $\frac{1}{2}$ pint hot vegetable water or stock (which can be made from a bouillon cube). Stir thoroughly until all the sediment is scraped from the tin and the gravy is a rich brown; return the pan to the heat and boil for 2–3 minutes. Serve very hot.

To make a thick gravy, leave 2 tbsps. of the fat in the tin, add 2 level tbsps. flour (if this is shaken from a flour dredger it gives a smoother result), blend well and cook over the heat until it turns brown, stirring continuously. Carefully mix in $\frac{1}{2}$ pint hot stock, boil for 2–3 minutes, season well, strain and serve very hot.

Greasy gravy, due to not draining off enough fat, or thin gravy, due to adding too much liquid, can be corrected by adding more flour, although this weakens the flavour.

If the sauce is very pale, extra colouring can be added in the form of gravy browning or caramel (made by heating sugar in an old spoon).

Meat extracts, which are sometimes added to give extra taste, overpower the characteristic meat flavour. However, a sliced carrot and onion cooked with the joint in the gravy will give extra 'body' to the taste without impairing it; 1 tbsp. cider or wine added at the last moment does wonders.

BLENDED
SAUCE

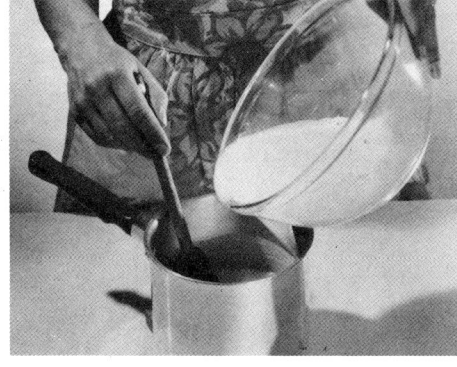

BREAD
SAUCE

MINT
SAUCE

Sauces and Stuffings

Stuffings

A good stuffing greatly enhances the flavour of the dish it accompanies and helps to make meat or poultry go further.

Stuffing may if preferred be cooked in a separate dish; this is frequently done when it is served with a piece of meat which has not been boned. Put the stuffing in a greased tin or dish and cook it for about 30 minutes in the oven, at the same time as the meat.

Forcemeat

4 oz. fresh breadcrumbs
1–2 oz. bacon or ham, chopped
1 level tbsp. chopped parsley
2 oz. suet
Rind of ½ a lemon, grated
½ level tsp. mixed herbs
Salt and pepper
Beaten egg

Mix all the ingredients together with a little beaten egg until the stuffing binds well.
Used with meat, poultry, fish and liver.

Sage and Onion

2 large onions
1 oz. butter
4 oz. fresh breadcrumbs
2 level tsps. dried sage
Salt and pepper

Chop the onions finely, cook until tender in boiling salted water, then drain. Combine with the remaining ingredients and mix well.
Used with roast goose, duck and pork.

Sausage

1 large onion, chopped
1 lb. pork sausage-meat
1 oz. lard
2 level tsps. chopped parsley
1 level tsp. mixed herbs
1 oz. fresh breadcrumbs (optional)
Salt and pepper

Mix the onion with the sausage-meat. Melt the lard and fry the sausage-meat and onion lightly for 2–3 minutes. Add the rest of the ingredients and mix well.
Used with chicken and turkey.

Mushroom

1 oz. margarine
4 oz. mushrooms, chopped
1 small onion, chopped
1 level tbsp. chopped parsley
Salt and pepper
2 oz. fresh breadcrumbs
Beaten egg

Melt the margarine and fry the mushrooms and onion lightly for 2–3 minutes. Add the parsley, seasoning and breadcrumbs and bind with a little beaten egg.
Used to stuff vegetables, such as tomatoes and green peppers.

Celery

4 oz. cooked celery, chopped
4 oz. fresh breadcrumbs
2 oz. suet
Rind of ½ a lemon, grated
1 level tbsp. chopped parsley
Salt and pepper
A little beaten egg or milk

Mix the celery with the crumbs, suet, lemon rind and parsley. Season and bind together with a little beaten egg and milk.
Used with white fish.

Bacon or Ham

½ oz. dripping
½ small onion, chopped
2 mushrooms, chopped
4 oz. chopped cooked bacon or ham
2 oz. fresh breadcrumbs
Salt and pepper
A little dry mustard
A few drops of Worcestershire sauce
Beaten egg or milk to bind

Melt the fat, fry the onion and add the mushrooms and bacon or ham. Mix well, then remove from the heat and add the crumbs, seasonings and sauce and bind with beaten egg or milk.
Used as a stuffing for vegetables, tomatoes, small marrows, peppers, etc.

Apple and Prune

4 oz. cooked rice
4 oz. stewed, stoned and quartered prunes
8 oz. cooking apples roughly chopped
2 oz. suet
2 oz. blanched and shredded almonds
Salt and pepper
Juice and grated rind of ½ a lemon
1 egg

Mix the rice, fruit, suet and nuts, season to taste, add the lemon juice and rind and bind with beaten egg.
Used for pork.

Forcemeat Stuffing

Grating bread, chopping parsley and binding mixture with beaten egg

Sage and Onion Stuffing

Two stages of chopping onions and addition of the sage to the mixture

Pastry

There is no room for guesswork in pastry-making—the ingredients must be in the correct proportions and mixed to the correct consistency. Cool working conditions and a hot oven are usually essential and the dough should be handled as little as possible—over-kneading gives a tough, hard result.

Plain flour is usually recommended; if self-raising is used, it gives a more open and spongy texture. A variety of fats (including butter, margarine and lard, or a combination) can be used for shortcrust, but for richer pastries it is better to use the fat recommended in the particular recipe. Proprietary vegetable shortenings are excellent; follow the makers' directions, as they sometimes advise using less fat to flour than in standard recipes.

Avoid using too much flour on board and rolling pin, as this alters the proportions. Take care also with the liquid—too much makes the pastry tough.

Shortcrust Pastry

8 oz. plain flour
½ level tsp. salt
2 oz. margarine
2 oz. lard
Cold water to mix

Sift the flour and salt into a basin. Cut the fats into the flour and complete the mixing by rubbing in with the finger-tips, until no lumps of fat remain. Add just enough cold water to bind the mixture, mixing with a round-bladed knife until it is evenly distributed. Draw the pastry together with the finger-tips to form a stiff dough; knead lightly until smooth. Turn it on to a lightly floured board and roll out and use as required.

Note: "6 oz. shortcrust pastry" means pastry made with 6 oz. flour and other ingredients in proportion. With ready-made pastries, the amount means weight as bought.

*Sifting flour and salt,
rubbing fat, adding water,
kneading together*

Plate Apple Pie

1 lb. cooking apples
6 oz. shortcrust pastry
4 oz. Demerara sugar
4 cloves
Egg or milk to glaze

Heat the oven to hot (425°F. mark 7). Peel and slice the apples. Roll out half the pastry and line the bottom of a 7-inch pie plate. Fill the plate with the sliced apples, sprinkle with the sugar and add the cloves. Roll out the remaining half of the pastry to make the top crust of the pie. Brush the edge of the bottom layer of pastry with water, put on the lid and seal well. Mark the edges with a knife and crimp together. Brush with beaten egg or milk. Bake towards the top of the oven for 15–20 minutes, then lower the temperature to moderate (350° F., mark 4) and cook for a further 15–20 minutes, or until the apple is cooked (test with a thin skewer).

Lining plate with pastry; adding filling; covering pie; decorating edges

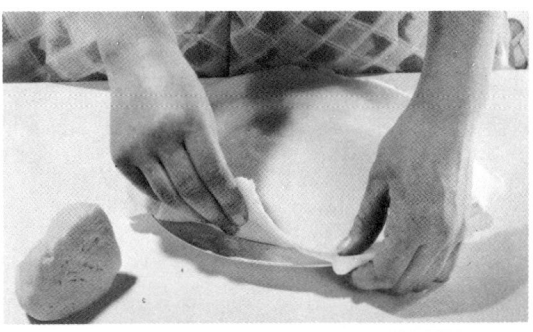

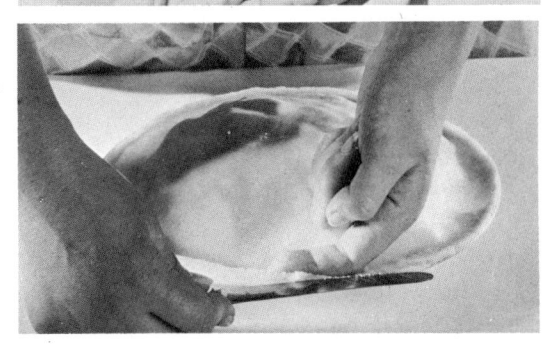

Pastry

Jam Tarts

6 oz. shortcrust pastry   Jam to fill
  (see page 92)

Heat the oven to hot (425°F., mark 7). Roll out the pastry fairly thinly, then cut out rounds with a 2½-inch fluted cutter. Ease the rounds into the tartlet tins and prick the base. Fill each pastry case one-third full with jam and bake towards the top of the oven for 10–15 minutes. Cool on a rack.

These tartlet cases can also be filled with lemon curd, mincemeat, marmalade and so on.

Individual Custard Tartlets

Line the patty tins with pastry. Whisk 2 eggs and 1 oz. sugar into ½ pint milk, pour this mixture into the tarts and sprinkle grated nutmeg on top. Bake in a fairly hot oven (375°F., mark 5) for 15–20 minutes.

Making and filling shortcrust pastry tartlet cases

Syrup Tart

4 oz. shortcrust pastry (see page 92)
3–4 tbsps. golden syrup
2 oz. fresh breadcrumbs
Grated rind of ½ a lemon

Heat the oven to hot (425°F., mark 7). Roll out the pastry thinly and line a 7-inch pie plate. Cut the edge at 1-inch intervals and fold over as shown. Mix together the syrup, breadcrumbs and lemon rind. Spread this mixture into the pastry case, keeping the border free. Cut 2 thin strips of pastry from the trimmings and make a cross. Cook towards the top of the oven for 15–20 minutes until golden-brown.

Variations

1. Replace the breadcrumbs by cake crumbs—use up stale sponge or even plain cakes, crumbling them finely. Any surplus can be stored in a small screw-top jar.
2. Replace the crumbs by crumbled cornflakes or breakfast cereal. (Even slightly stale ones can be used).
3. For a richer mixture, mix a beaten egg in with the filling ingredients.

Decorating the edge of the pastry, adding the filling and putting the pastry cross in position

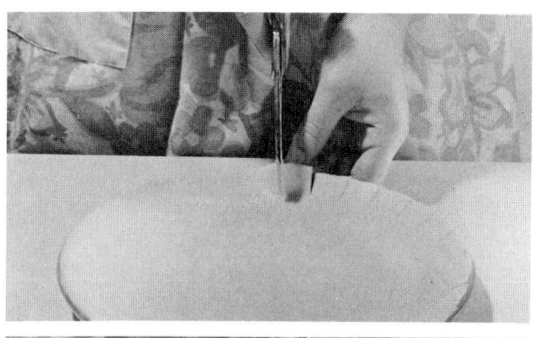

Pastry

Opposite: lining a foil case with pastry, crimping the edge, filling with baking beans and removing paper and beans after baking blind

Flans

Flans may be made with ordinary shortcrust pastry (see page 92), but for those with a fruit or similar filling, a special richer, sweetened mixture may be made—see recipe below.

Special flan rings, both plain and fluted, are sold in several sizes. To use them, stand them on a baking sheet. If no special ring is to hand, use a sandwich cake tin or a deep pie plate.

Flan Pastry

4 oz. plain flour
2 oz. margarine, lard, mixed
1 level tsp. caster sugar
1 egg yolk
Cold water to mix

Heat the oven to fairly hot (400°F., mark 6). Make as for shortcrust pastry, page 92, using the egg yolk and a little water to bind the mixture.

Making and filling a flan

Turn the pastry on to a board and roll out to the size of the flan case, ring or tin. Ease the pastry into the case, fold the edge under and crimp to give a high border. Bake blind as described below.

Meanwhile, prepare a filling. For the flan shown here, drain a can of fruit.

When the flan case is quite cold, arrange the fruit in it neatly and cover with fruit glaze (see below.)

Baking Blind

Baking Blind—this is a term used to describe the cooking of a pastry case or shell without a filling. To keep the case a good shape, cover the surface of the uncooked pastry with a round of greased greaseproof paper, greased side down, then fill with some dried beans or peas kept specially for this purpose. Bake in a fairly hot oven (400°F., mark 6) for 15 minutes. Remove the beans and paper and return the flan case to the oven for 10 minutes to allow the pastry to dry out. Remove from the oven and cool.

Pastry cases which have been baked blind may be stored in a tin when cold and kept until required. Fill them with fruit or any suitable sweet or savoury mixture and garnish or decorate as preferred.

Glaze for fruit Flans

2-3 level tsps. arrowroot
¼ pint strained fruit juice
Sugar if needed
Lemon juice (optional)
2 level tsps. red-currant jelly or apricot jam (optional)
Colouring, if required

Blend the arrowroot with a little of the fruit juice. Put the rest of the juice and the sugar into a saucepan and boil until the syrup is quite clear and of a coating consistency. Add a squeeze of lemon juice, the jelly or jam and the colouring (if used). The syrup should be well flavoured and of a fairly thick consistency—if too thin, it will soak into the pastry and make it sodden. It must be used while still warm, as it sets quite quickly.

Crumb Crusts

These quickly prepared crusts, usually made from biscuit or similar crumbs, are a good way of using up biscuits that have lost their first crispness.

6 oz. plain biscuits (e.g., wheatmeal)
1 level tbsp. sugar
3 oz. butter

Crush the biscuits with a rolling pin and mix with the sugar. Melt the butter and mix with the crumbs until they bind together. Put the mixture in a greased shallow pie plate or sandwich cake tin, spreading it evenly over the base and up the sides; press firmly into place. Leave in a cool place until set.

If the flan is to be eaten at once, fill with fresh, cooked or canned fruit, as above. Alternatively, use a packet pudding mixture, adding if you like some diced fruit—for instance, diced canned pineapple used with a pineapple-flavoured mix.

Variations:
1. Replace the biscuits by crushed cornflakes—add a pinch of ground cinnamon to flavour, if you like.
2. Omit the sugar and fat and bind the crumbs with 3-4 oz. chocolate, melted with a knob of butter.

Opposite: Putting in the fruit filling, making and adding the glaze

Making a Flan Case

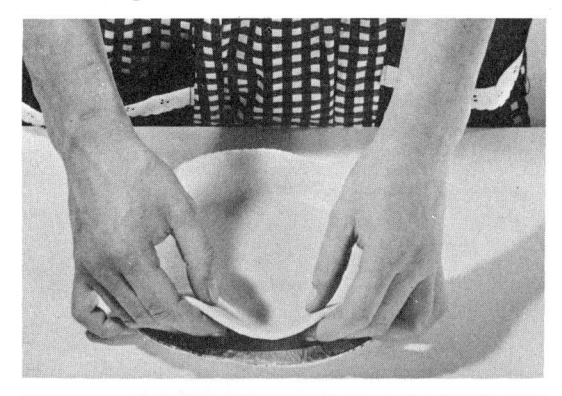

Filling a Flan Case

Pastry

Apricot Amber

4 oz. flan pastry (see page 96)
1 15½ oz. can of apricots
2 eggs, separated
2 oz. butter, melted
2 oz. caster sugar

Heat the oven to hot (425°F., mark 7). Roll out the pastry and line a metal pie plate or foil dish; trim the edges and crimp. Bake blind towards the top of the oven for 15 minutes, remove the paper and beans and return the case to the oven for a further 5 minutes to dry out. Remove from the oven and cool. Reduce the oven heat to moderate (350°F., mark 4).

Drain the apricots, then sieve them to make a pulp. Stir the egg yolks and melted butter into the apricot pulp and pour into the cooked flan case. Cook in the centre of the oven for 15 minutes, or until the filling is firm. Whisk the egg whites and fold in the sugar; pile on to the apricot filling. Reduce the oven heat to cool (300°F., mark 1), put the Apricot Amber towards the bottom of the oven and cook for 15-20 minutes, until the meringue topping is crisp. Glacé cherries and angelica may be used as decoration—see colour picture facing page 144.

Draining and sieving fruit, stirring in melted butter and egg yolks; topping the filling with meringue

Fruit Lattice Pie

1 lb. cooking apples (or other fruit)
4 oz. flour
2 level tsps. ground cinnamon
2 oz. fat
Cold water
1 oz. butter
2 oz. brown sugar
2 oz. raisins

Heat the oven to hot (425°F., mark 7). Peel, core and slice the apples. Sift the flour and 1 tsp. cinnamon and rub in the fat until the mixture resembles fine breadcrumbs. Add enough cold water to bind the mixture to a stiff dough. Roll out the pastry and line an 8-inch pie plate with it. Trim and decorate the edges, keeping the trimmings. Bake this pastry case blind for 15 minutes, towards the top of the oven; remove the paper and return the case to the oven to dry out—about 5 minutes. Gently simmer the apples, butter, sugar, raisins and remaining 1 tsp. cinnamon together, until the apples are soft and pulpy. Pour this apple filling into the cooked pastry case. Roll out the pastry trimmings into an oblong, cut into thin strips and use these to make a lattice over the top of the pie. Return the pie to the oven and bake for a further 10–15 minutes, until the latticework is set. This pie can be served hot or cold.

Flavouring the apples, filling the pastry case, cutting and adding pastry strips for a lattice

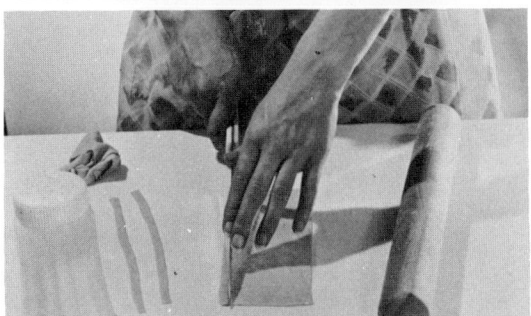

Pastry

Mince Pies

| 1 pkt. bought flaky pastry | 1 egg, beaten |
| Mincemeat | Icing or caster sugar to dredge (optional) |

Heat the oven to hot (425°F., mark 7). Roll out the pastry to the thickness of a penny (1/16th inch). Cut 2½-inch rounds with a plain cutter and cut the same number of rounds with a 2-inch plain cutter. Fit the larger rounds into the patty tins and put 1 tsp. of mincemeat in each. Brush the edges with water. Place the smaller rounds on top and seal. Make a small hole in the top of each pie and glaze with beaten egg. Bake towards the top of the oven for 15–20 minutes. Remove from the tins and cool. If you like, dredge the mince pies with sugar before serving.

Preparing the pastry cases and lids, adding the filling, covering the pies

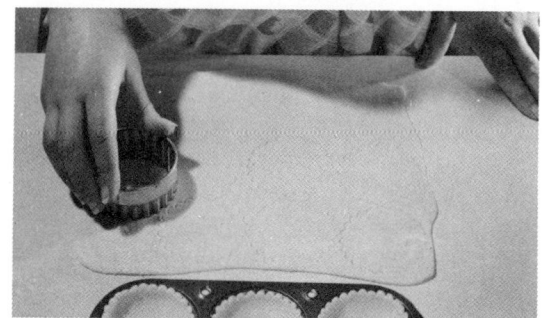

Sausage Rolls

1 small pkt. bought flaky pastry
8 oz. sausage-meat
Egg to glaze

Heat the oven to fairly hot (400°F., mark 6). Roll out the pastry to about the thickness of a penny (1/16th inch); make it into an oblong 6 inches wide and cut this into two. Divide the sausage-meat into 2 portions and dust each lightly with flour. Roll into 2 "sausages" the length of the strips of pastry. Lay a roll of sausage down the centre of each strip, brush each side of the pastry with egg, then fold one side of the pastry over the meat. Press the two edges firmly together and seal by making horizontal cuts with a knife. Cut into pieces 1½–2 inches long, place on a baking tray and cook towards the top of the oven for 30 minutes.

Cutting the pastry, rolling the sausage-meat, brushing the pastry with milk and sealing the edges

Batters

Standard Batter Mixture

4 oz. plain flour
A pinch of salt
1 egg
½ pint milk and water mixed

Sift the flour and salt into a mixing bowl and make a well in the centre. Pour the egg and 2 tbsps. of the liquid into the well. Using a wooden spoon and working from the centre, gradually mix some of the flour from the edges into the egg and milk and beat well until smooth. Gradually add ¼ pint of the liquid, beating gently and drawing in the rest of the flour until all is mixed in and the batter is smooth and bubbly. Stir in the remaining liquid.

Use for Pancakes, Yorkshire Pudding, Toad in the Hole and similar dishes (see recipes on following pages).

Sifting the flour and salt, adding the egg, beating in half the liquid and stirring in the remaining liquid

Coating Batter

4 oz. plain flour
A pinch of salt
1 egg
¼ pint milk and water mixed

Make in the same way as the standard batter mixture above, but add all the liquid at once, then beat until smooth and bubbly. Use for coating apple rings, pieces of fish, etc., which are to be fried—see Fritter recipe on page 105 and Fish in Batter on page 28.

Pancakes

4 oz. plain flour
A pinch of salt
1 egg
½ pint milk and water, mixed

A little lard
Caster sugar
1 lemon, cut into wedges

Make the batter mixture (see opposite). Melt just enough lard in a thick frying pan to coat the bottom and sides, then pour off any surplus. When the fat is hot, pour in a little batter—just enough to cover the bottom of the pan. Cook the pancake until it is golden-brown on the underside, then toss or turn it over and cook the second side. Turn out onto a plate, sprinkle with sugar, cover with another plate and keep warm under the grill or in a cool oven whilst the rest are being made. When all the pancakes are cooked, roll them up singly and serve with wedges of lemon.

Draining off surplus fat, pouring in batter for one pancake and frying first on one side, then on the other

Batters

*Use the same batter for
Yorkshire Pudding and Popovers,
but cook it in one large tin
or several small ones respectively*

Yorkshire Pudding

Make ½ pint standard batter mixture (page 102). Heat the oven to hot (425°F., mark 7). Put a little lard or dripping into a shallow tin and heat in the oven. Pour in the batter and bake near the top of the oven for 35–40 minutes. Cut into squares and serve with roast beef.

Popovers

Make ½ pint standard batter mixture. Heat the oven to hot (425°F., mark 7). Put a little lard or dripping into some patty tins, heat in the oven, then pour some batter into each tin. Bake near the top of the oven for 15–20 minutes. Serve with roast beef.

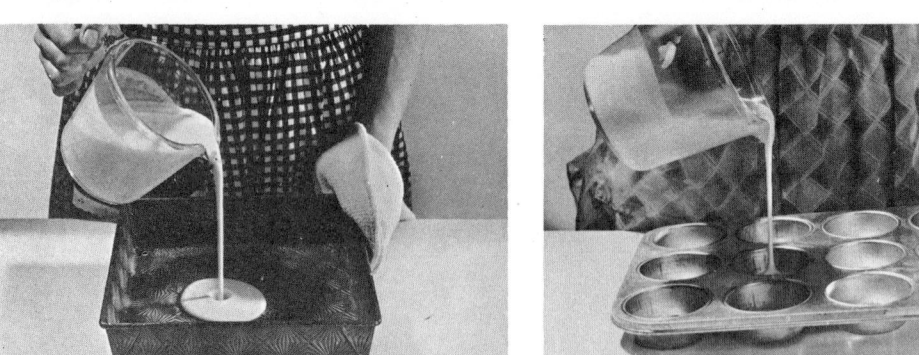

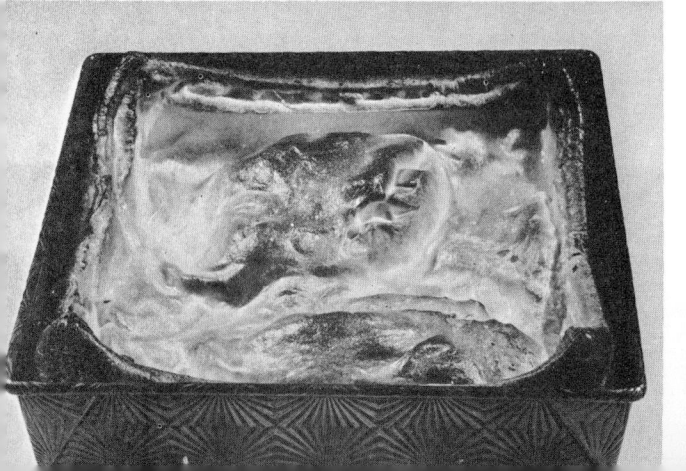

Apple Fritters

¼ pint coating batter
1 lb. cooking apples, peeled
Deep fat for frying
Caster sugar and cinnamon

Make the batter as in recipe on page 102, making sure it is of a coating consistency. Slice the apples and remove the cores. (A small cutter may be used, if available.) Coat each piece with the batter and let it drain before frying. Heat the deep fat. To see if it is hot enough drop in a 1-inch cube of stale bread—it should take 60–70 seconds to brown. Cook the fritters until they are golden-brown all over, turning them once. Drain well on crumpled kitchen paper and serve sprinkled with sugar and cinnamon.

Apples are the most usual fruit to use for fritters, but quartered bananas, sections of orange or tangerine and sliced pineapple may also be used.

Savoury fritters may be made in the same way, using slices of corned beef, luncheon meat, etc. The batter mixture should be suitably seasoned and a little finely chopped onion may be included.

Making the batter, coring and coating the apple rings and deep-frying

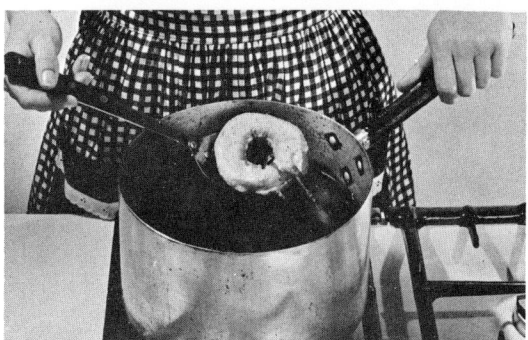

Batters

Toad in the Hole

½ pint standard batter (page 102)
Lard or dripping
1 lb. sausages

Heat the oven to hot (425°F., mark 7). Put the fat and sausages in a fairly large shallow tin and heat in the oven, then pour in the batter (or put in batter and add sausages) and bake near top of oven for about ¾–1 hour.

Baked Fruit Batter

1 lb. cooking apples (or other fruit)
½ pint standard batter
1 oz. butter
Rind of ½ a lemon, grated
3–4 oz. sugar

Prepare the fruit as necessary. Heat the oven to hot (425°F., mark 7).
Make the batter (see page 102). Heat the butter in a fairly deep tin. Put the fruit into the tin and sprinkle with the lemon rind and the sugar, pour in the batter and bake near the top of the oven for about ¾ hour.

Combining batter with sausages and fruit respectively to make Toad in the Hole and Baked Fruit Batter

Hot Puddings

Stuffed Baked Apples

4 even-sized cooking apples
3–4 oz. mixed dried fruit
1 oz. Demerara sugar
½ oz. butter
2 tbsps. water

Heat the oven to fairly hot (400°F., mark 6). Remove the centres from the apples with a corer and make a cut in the skin round the middle of each apple. Put them in an ovenproof dish. Fill the holes with the mixed fruit and sugar. Put a knob of butter on each apple and pour the water round them. Bake in the centre of the oven for about 45 minutes, until the fruit is cooked.

Variations
1. Replace the Demerara sugar with golden syrup, honey or white sugar.
2. Include marmalade, mincemeat, chopped dates, almonds, walnuts or crystallised ginger in the filling.
3. When the apples are cooked, remove the skin above the cut and cover them with a meringue mixture made from 2 egg whites and 4 oz. caster sugar. Replace in the oven until lightly browned.

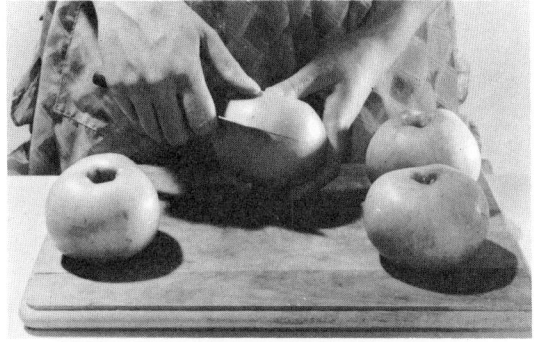

Coring and slitting the apples, stuffing and adding the water

Hot Puddings

Milk Puddings

Rice Pudding

1½ oz. rice   1 pint milk
2 oz. sugar   Ground nutmeg

Heat the oven to cool (300°F., mark 2). Wash the rice in a sieve under the tap. Put into a greased ovenproof dish, with the sugar and milk, sprinkle with nutmeg and bake for 2–2½ hours, stirring once or twice.
Tapioca is cooked in the same way.

Semolina Pudding

1 pint milk   2–3 oz. sugar
1 oz. semolina

Heat the oven to moderate (350°F., mark 4). Warm the milk gently, then sprinkle in the semolina and the sugar; continue heating, stirring all the time, until the mixture thickens. Pour into an ovenproof dish and bake in the oven until the top is brown.
Fine sago and ground rice are cooked in the same way.

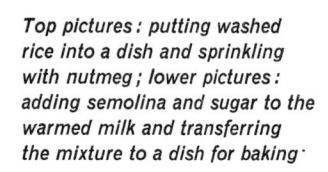

Top pictures: putting washed rice into a dish and sprinkling with nutmeg; lower pictures: adding semolina and sugar to the warmed milk and transferring the mixture to a dish for baking.

Baked Egg Custard Tart

4 oz. plain flour	2 eggs
A pinch of salt	1 level tbsp. sugar
1 oz. margarine	½ pint milk
1 oz. lard	Grated or ground
Water to mix	nutmeg

Heat the oven to hot (425°F., mark 7). Make the shortcrust pastry with the flour, salt, margarine, lard and water (see page 92). Roll out so that it is 1 inch larger all round than a 7-inch pie plate; line the plate, trim off any excess pastry, damp the edges and fold ½ inch of the pastry under all the way round. Crimp the edges with the fingers. Beat the eggs lightly and add the sugar. Warm the milk slightly and pour it on to the sweetened eggs. Pour this mixture through a sieve into the pastry case. Sprinkle with a little nutmeg and bake in the centre of the oven for 10–15 minutes, until the pastry is set, then reduce the heat to warm (325°F., mark 3) and cook for a further 20–30 minutes, or until the custard is set.

Baked Custard—cook the custard mixture in a greased pie dish; stand the dish in a deep baking tin and pour cold water round it to prevent over-heating. Bake in a cool oven (300°F., mark 2) until it is set and lightly coloured—about 45 minutes.

Crimping the edge of the pastry case, making and adding the custard filling and sprinkling with nutmeg

109

Hot Puddings

Suetcrust Pastry

8 oz. self-raising flour
1 level tsp. salt
4 oz. shredded suet
8 tbsps. cold water (approx.)

Mix together the flour, salt and suet. Add enough cold water to give a light, elastic dough and knead very lightly until smooth. Roll out to ¼ inch thickness.
This pastry may be used for both sweet and savoury dishes and can be steamed, boiled or baked; the first two are the most satisfactory methods, as baked suetcrust pastry is inclined to be hard.

Jam Roly-Poly

8 oz. suetcrust pastry　　　　Jam

Put some water in a steamer and bring to the boil. Roll out the pastry into an oblong shape, keeping the edges straight. Spread generously with jam to within 1 inch of the edges. Moisten the edges of the pastry with cold water and roll it up as tightly as possible. Wrap in greaseproof paper and roll in a pudding cloth or foil. Steam for 2-2½ hours, or boil for 1½ hours.

Shaping the pastry, spreading with jam, rolling up and tying in a cloth

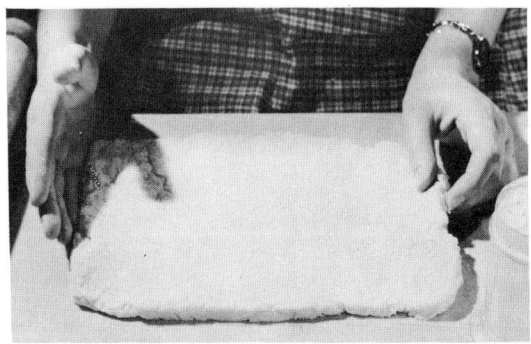

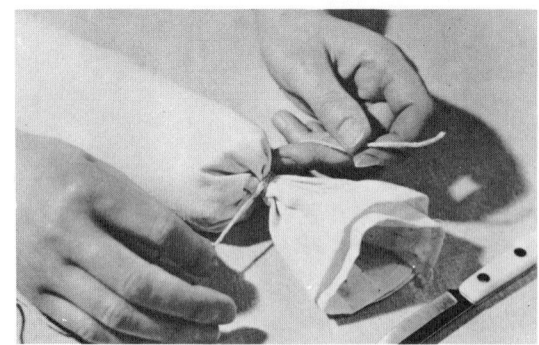

Fruit Layer Pudding

8 oz. suetcrust pastry
1 lb. prepared rhubarb
4 oz. sugar

Variations—Use:
1. Sliced apples with grated orange rind.
2. Golden syrup with breadcrumbs.
3. Halved plums, damsons, cherries or gooseberries.

Put some water in a steamer and bring to the boil. Cut a double piece of greaseproof paper 2-3 inches larger all round than the top of a 1½-pint pudding basin; grease the centre of the paper and the inside of the basin. Divide the pastry into 4 portions; roll each piece out separately, graduating the sizes to fit the basin. Place the smallest piece in the basin and put a layer of fruit and sugar over it. Continue in this way until all the fruit and pastry have been used, finishing with a layer of pastry. Cover the top of the pudding with the piece of greaseproof paper and a cloth or foil, then steam for about 2 hours. When the pudding is cooked, turn it out carefully, loosening the edges with a knife.

Rolling out the pastry, putting alternate layers of pastry and filling in a basin, adding top layer and covering basin

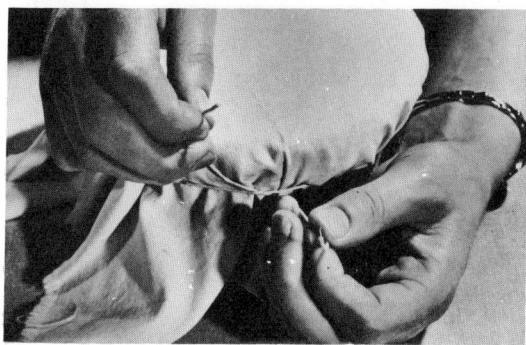

Hot Puddings

Steamed Fruit Pudding

4 oz. flour
2 level tsps. baking powder
½ level tsp. salt
2 level tsps. mixed spice
2 oz. sugar
4 oz. fresh breadcrumbs
4 oz. shredded suet
6 oz. mixed dried fruit
¼ pint milk

Put some water in a steamer and bring to the boil. Grease a 1½-pint pudding basin well. Sift together the dry ingredients, add the crumbs and then the suet; if necessary rub this in slightly to distribute it evenly. Stir in the fruit. Make a well in the centre and add the milk, mixing to a dropping consistency. Turn the mixture into the pudding basin, cover with greased foil and secure with string. Steam over rapidly boiling water for 2–2½ hours.

Combining the dry ingredients, adding the liquid and putting the mixture into a basin

Steamed Jam Sponge

2 level tbsps. jam, syrup or marmalade
3 oz. margarine
3 oz. caster sugar
1 egg, beaten
5 oz. self-raising flour, sifted
2 tbsps. milk to mix (approx.)

Put some water in a steamer and bring to the boil. Put the jam in the bottom of the basin. Cream the fat and sugar with a wooden spoon until pale and fluffy; add the beaten egg gradually, beating well after each addition. Fold in half the flour with a tablespoon, then fold in the remainder, adding sufficient milk to make the mixture soft enough to drop quite easily from the spoon when this is held above the bowl and shaken. Put the mixture into the basin, so that it is only two-thirds full, and level the top. Cover the basin with greaseproof paper or foil and tie with string. Steam for 2 hours, remove the paper, loosen the edges of the pudding with a knife and turn it out on to a serving dish—see colour picture facing page 129.

Greasing the basin and covering paper, putting in the jam and the pudding mixture and covering the basin

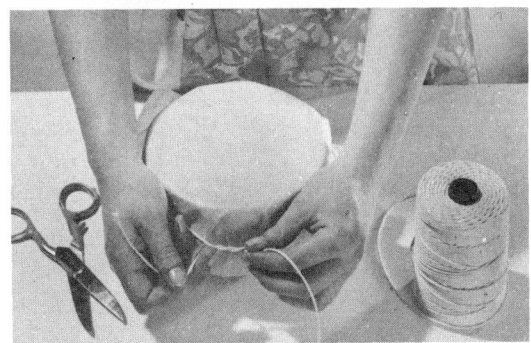

Hot Puddings

Rich Christmas Pudding

6 oz. almonds
1 lb. 4 oz. stoned raisins
12 oz. currants
8 oz. sultanas
4 oz. mixed peel
4 oz. glacé cherries
8 oz. peeled and cored apple
Grated rind and juice of 1 lemon and 1 orange
12 oz. plain flour
1 level tsp. salt
2 level tsps. mixed spice
12 oz. fresh breadcrumbs
12 oz. shredded suet
8 oz. caster sugar
8 oz. soft brown sugar
4 tbsps. brandy
4 eggs
¼ pint milk, approx.

Grease 3 pudding basins—1-pint, 1½-pint and 2-pint. Blanch the almonds and when they are cool enough remove the skins, then dry the nuts. Wash and dry the fruit thoroughly, or rub it in flour on a sieve to remove any small stalks, etc. Chop the nuts, peel, cherries and apple and mix with the fruit and the lemon and orange rind. Add the mixture to the flour, salt, spice, breadcrumbs, suet and sugars.

Mix together the fruit juices, brandy and eggs and mix very thoroughly with the dry ingredients, adding enough milk to give a dropping consistency.

Turn the mixture into the prepared basins and cover with greaseproof paper and a pudding cloth or foil. Either steam or boil in a saucepan with water coming halfway up the basins. Allow the following times:

1-pint pudding—about 5 hours
1½-pint pudding—about 7 hours
2-pint pudding—about 9 hours

When the puddings are cool, remove the pudding cloths and replace by new ones. The puddings will keep for 4 months. Before serving, cook again for the following times:

1-pint pudding—2 hours
1½-pint pudding—3 hours
2-pint pudding—3 hours.

Economical Christmas Pudding

4 oz. sultanas
2 oz. currants
4 oz. stoned raisins
5 oz. flour
½ level tsp. salt
3 oz. fresh breadcrumbs
3 oz. suet or cooking fat
3 oz. sugar
1 level tsp. mixed spice
A little grated nutmeg
2 eggs, beaten
1 oz. syrup
1 level tbsp. marmalade
A little milk or water
A few drops of vanilla essence
A few drops of almond essence
A little browning

Grease 1 medium-sized or 2 small basins. Wash and pick over the dried fruits. Put the flour, salt and breadcrumbs into a bowl. If suet is used, add this; if cooking fat is used, rub it into the flour and breadcrumb mixture. Add the sugar and spices and mix well. Add the dried fruits, then the eggs, syrup, marmalade and enough milk or water to give a soft dropping consistency. Stir in the vanilla and almond essences and enough browning to colour it lightly. Put into the basin or basins, nearly filling them, cover with greased greaseproof paper and foil and steam for about 6 hours. Steam for a further 2 hours before serving.

This pudding will keep for 3–4 weeks.

Pictures opposite show blanching almonds, cleaning dried fruit, grating lemon rind, mixing the dry ingredients, filling and covering the basins

115

Hot Puddings

Rhubarb Crumble

1 lb. rhubarb	6 oz. plain flour
6 oz. sugar	1 level tbsp. Demerara
3 oz. margarine	for topping

Heat the oven to moderate (350°F., mark 4). Cut the sticks of rhubarb into pieces and put in an ovenproof dish; add 3 oz. of the sugar. Rub the fat into the flour until the texture resembles breadcrumbs. Add the remaining sugar and mix together; sprinkle on top of the rhubarb. Finally sprinkle on the Demerara sugar and bake in the centre of the oven for 40–45 minutes.

If you are using a soft fruit, or one that has been already stewed, cook the crumble towards the top of a fairly hot oven (375°F., mark 5) for about 20 minutes.

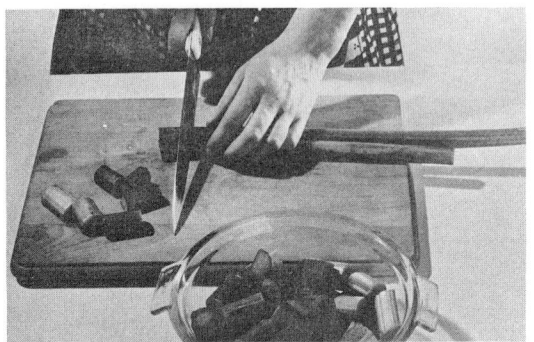

Preparing the rhubarb, making and adding the crumble mixture and topping with brown sugar

Fruit Cobbler

8 oz. self-raising flour
A pinch of salt
2 oz. butter or margarine
2 oz. sugar
1 egg, beaten
1–2 tbsps. milk
1 lb. 4 oz. can of plums

Heat the oven to hot (425°F., mark 7). Sieve the flour and salt together and rub in the fat until the mixture is like fine breadcrumbs. Stir in the sugar. Add the egg and enough milk to make the mixture bind together. Knead to a smooth, fairly soft dough. Turn on to a floured board, roll out $\frac{1}{2}$ inch thick and cut into 2-inch rounds or scones. Drain the plums, heat well, pour into the dish and place the scones on the fruit in a ring round the edge of the dish, slightly overlapping. Brush with a little milk, and bake near the top of the oven for 10–15 minutes, or until the rounds are golden-brown, well risen and firm to the touch.

Rolling out and cutting the dough, putting the plums and cobbler topping in the dish

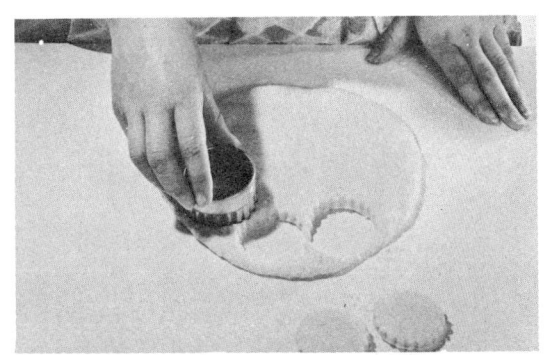

Hot Puddings

Apple Charlotte

3 oz. fresh breadcrumbs
2 oz. shredded suet
Grated rind and juice of 1 lemon
3–4 oz. Demerara sugar
1 lb. cooking apples, sliced
1 oz. butter

Heat the oven to moderate (350°F., mark 4). Grease an ovenproof dish. Mix together the breadcrumbs, suet, lemon rind and sugar. Put alternate layers of apple and the breadcrumb mixture into the dish. Sprinkle with a little of the lemon juice and finish with a layer of crumbs. Dot with butter and bake in the centre of oven for about 1 hour, until fruit is cooked.

Mixing the dry ingredients, putting alternate layers of apples and crumb mixture into a dish and topping with butter

Stewed Apples

1 lb. cooking apples   ¼ pint water
4 oz. sugar

Wipe the fruit, peel, core and cut into slices. Dissolve the sugar in the water, add the fruit to the syrup and simmer gently until tender, taking care not to break up the slices. Serve hot or cold.

Most fruits can be cooked in the same general way, but hard ones such as pears and some plums need a little more water, while very juicy ones of the berry type will need even less.

The first picture shows apples and the second, pears cut up for stewing

Cold Puddings

Jelly Whip

1 pkt. raspberry or strawberry jelly
1 small can of cherries

Make up the jelly, using the cherry juice and some water. Drain the cherries and put a few in the bottom of each individual glass. Pour on a little of the jelly and allow to set, then fill the glasses half-full with jelly and allow this to set. Let the remainder of the jelly set very lightly in the basin, then whisk until light and fluffy. When the jelly in the glasses is set, pile the whipped jelly on top. Serve decorated with cherries.

Jelly Variations

Many quick-and-easy cold sweets can be made up from a packet of jelly. Here are some suggestions:

1. When making the jelly, replace some of the water by syrup from a can of fruit; set in the usual way or whip as in the first recipe. As a further variation, some of the fruit may be chopped and folded in before the jelly is set.
2. When whipping the jelly as in the first recipe, add the contents of a small can of cream. Set as usual.
3. Make up 2 half-packets of contrasting coloured jellies. Layer them alternately into glasses, remembering to let one layer set before adding the next.
4. Whip the jellies as in the first recipe before setting them in layers.
5. Make up a lemon jelly and leave to set in a bowl. Whip up 2 egg whites and fold into the almost-set jelly. Put into glasses and serve decorated with grated chocolate.
6. This depends on you having a small can of ready-prepared evaporated milk (see this page). Make up an orange jelly in the usual way and put to set in a bowl. When it is on the point of setting, whip in the prepared evaporated milk. Pile the mixture in glasses and decorate with some sliced crystallised orange.
To prepare evaporated milk for use in this kind of pudding, boil it in its can in a pan of water for 20 minutes, leave to cool and then chill it. If you do 2 or 3 at a time, they can be kept in the refrigerator for a long time, ready for immediate use.
7. For children, set an ordinary jelly in a shallow tin (e.g., a meat tin). To serve, cut it into cubes and pile into glasses with some ice-cream, cream or fruit—fresh or canned.

Apricot Fool

1 15½ oz. can of apricots
¼ pint custard
¼ pint double cream
Chopped walnuts (optional)

Drain the apricots and sieve them to make a pulp. Add this pulp to the custard. Lightly whip the cream and fold into the mixture. Pile into glasses and decorate the top with chopped nuts, if used.

Fruit Fool is a very adaptable sweet that can be made from many types of fruit, though those with a strong colour look best, e.g. rhubarb, damsons, raspberries, blackberries and perhaps the most traditional of all, gooseberries.

For a more economical version, use all custard—for parties, increase the proportion of cream; the authentic old English recipe uses all cream, giving a gorgeous rich sweet.

Serve something crisp with fruit fool as a contrast to its smooth texture—for instance, plain sweet biscuits or sponge fingers.

Jelly Whip · Apricot Fool

Cold Puddings

Fruit Trifle

6 individual sponge cakes
Raspberry jam
1 glass sherry or
   fruit juice
2 bananas, sliced
2 peaches, sliced
¾ pint custard
¼ pint double cream
Chocolate vermicelli

Split the sponge cakes, spread with jam, cut into small pieces and place in the bottom of a large bowl. Pour the sherry or fruit juice over. Cover the cake with the mixed fruits. Pour the custard over the cake and fruit and allow to set. Pour on the double cream and sprinkle chocolate vermicelli round the edge.

Spreading cake with jam before putting in dish; adding fruit, then custard; decorating the top

Apple Cornflake Crunch

1 lb. cooking apples
2–3 oz. sugar
1½ oz. butter
2 tbsps. golden syrup
1 oz. cornflakes
4–6 tbsps. single cream

Peel, core and slice the apples, place in a saucepan with 2 tbsps. water and simmer until soft and pulpy. Stir in the sugar, making sure it is dissolved, then rub the mixture through a sieve. Stir the purée until smooth, then divide it between 4 glasses. Heat the butter and syrup in a pan until melted; stir in the cornflakes and mix until evenly coated. Pour a thin layer of cream on top of the apple in each dish, then pile the cornflake mixture on top.

Cooking and sieving the apples; preparing and adding the cornflake mixture

Cold Puddings

Fruit Salad

1 small can of pineapple pieces
4–6 oz. sugar
2 oz. black or white grapes
2 bananas, peeled
2 rosy-skinned eating apples
1 orange, skinned
1 pear, peeled

Open the can of pineapple, strain off the juice and make up to ½ pint with water. Place this with the sugar in a saucepan and heat slowly to dissolve the sugar; cool for a moment and pour into a glass bowl. Add all the fruits to the bowl, preparing them as necessary. Slice the bananas; cut the apples into quarters, remove the cores and cut into thin slices; slice the skinned orange across; cut the pear into thin slices; cut the grapes in half and remove the pips. Mix all together and leave to stand for a time before serving. Cream or ice cream is often served with a fruit salad.

Pouring the sweetened fruit syrup into the bowl; preparing and adding the various fruits

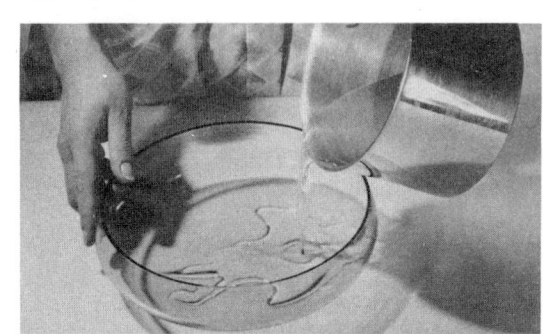

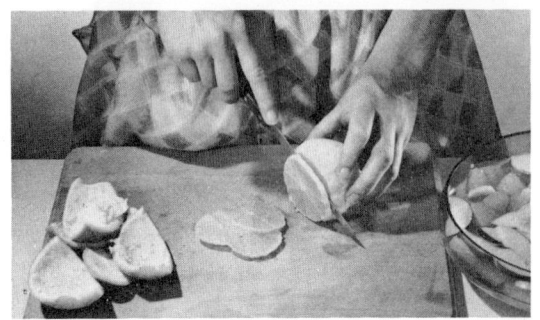

Peach Condé

A 15½ oz. can of creamed rice
4 peach halves
4 level tbsps. redcurrant jelly
2 tbsps. water
Juice of ½ a lemon

Divide the contents of the can of rice between 4 sundae glasses. Put a peach half in each. Make a sauce by heating the jelly, water and lemon juice together until thick and syrupy, then spoon this over the top of the peaches and rice.

Variations:

Separate 2 eggs and add the yolks to the rice in a pan. Heat gently, stirring all the time, until the mixture begins to bubble. Allow to cool, then pour into an ovenproof dish, Cover the top with a layer of melted raspberry jam. Whisk up the egg whites until stiff, gradually whisk in 1½ oz. caster sugar, fold in a further 1½ oz. sugar and pile this meringue on top of the jam. Crisp under a hot grill or in a hot oven (425°F., mark 7).

Putting the rice and the peach halves into the glasses; preparing and adding the sauce

Cold Puddings

Ice Cream

½ pint double cream or evaporated milk

¼ pint vanilla-flavoured custard

Set the refrigerator to the coldest setting. Whisk the cream or evaporated milk until it is thick and will hold a "trail". Fold into the cool custard, turn the mixture into a freezing tray and place in the refrigerator. When the ice cream has frozen (about 1 hour, depending on the refrigerator) turn it out from the tray into a bowl and whisk again. Return it to the ice tray and freeze until required. Spoon into glasses and serve with fruit or a sauce.

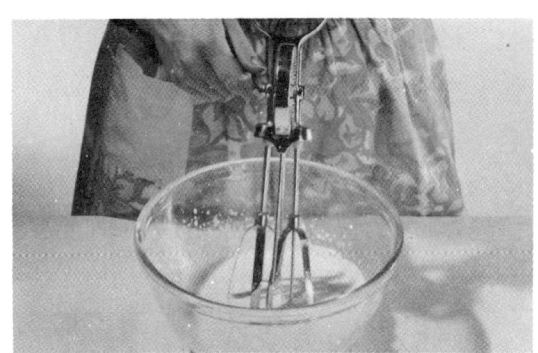

This page: whisking the cream or evaporated milk, putting into the freezing tray, re-whisking and serving. Opposite page: making up Banana Split and Pear Sundae

Banana Split

¼–½ pint jam sauce (see page 131)
Ice cream
4 bananas, peeled
1 oz. walnuts, chopped

Make the jam sauce. Place a portion of ice cream in each of 4 small, shallow dishes. Slice the bananas lengthways and put on either side of the ice cream. Spoon some jam sauce over and sprinkle with nuts.

Pear Sundae

Ice cream
8 canned pear halves
Chocolate sauce (see page 132)
¼ pint double cream, whipped
1 oz. walnuts, chopped

Place some ice cream in each of 4 sundae glasses. Place 2 pear halves on each portion, pour chocolate sauce over and spoon some cream on top. Sprinkle with chopped nuts.

Cold Puddings

Strawberry Shortcake

8 oz. self-raising flour
A pinch of salt
3 oz. margarine
3 oz. sugar
1 egg, beaten
1–2 tbsps. milk
¾–1 lb. strawberries
3–4 level tbsps. sugar
¼ pint double cream, whisked

Heat the oven to fairly hot (375°F., mark 5). Grease an 8-inch sandwich cake tin. Sift the flour and salt together and rub in the fat until the mixture resembles breadcrumbs; stir in the sugar. Add the egg a little at a time and a little milk, so that the mixture begins to stick together. Collect the mixture together with the hand and knead lightly into a smooth, fairly firm dough. Turn on to a floured board and roll out the dough into a round 8 inches across. Press the dough evenly into the cake tin and bake near the top of the oven for 20 minutes, or until golden and firm. Turn out of the tin on to a cooling tray. Wash the strawberries and remove the hulls and stems. Keep about a dozen berries for decorating; lightly crush the rest and sprinkle with 2–3 tbsps. sugar.

Split the shortcake, spread the lower half with the crushed fruit and replace the top. Add the remaining sugar to the cream and pile on the cake. Decorate with the whole berries—see colour picture opposite.

Other soft fruit may be used in the same way.

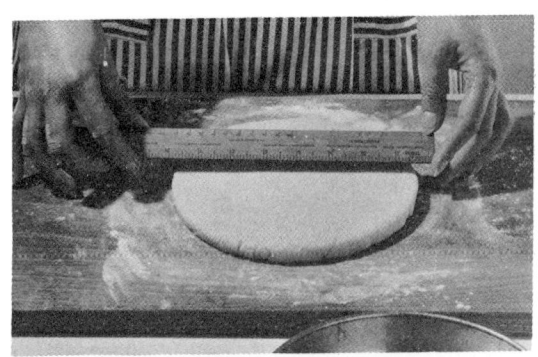

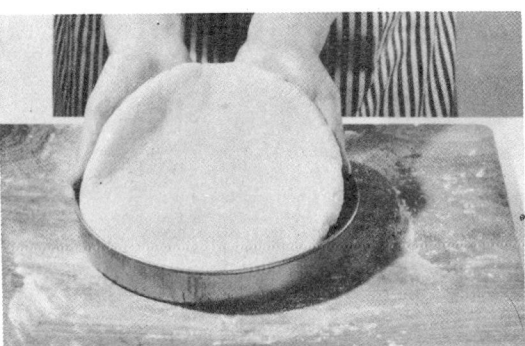

Rolling the dough into a round to fit the tin and putting it in; spreading the cooked and split cake with fruit; adding the topping

Strawberry Shortcake: opposite

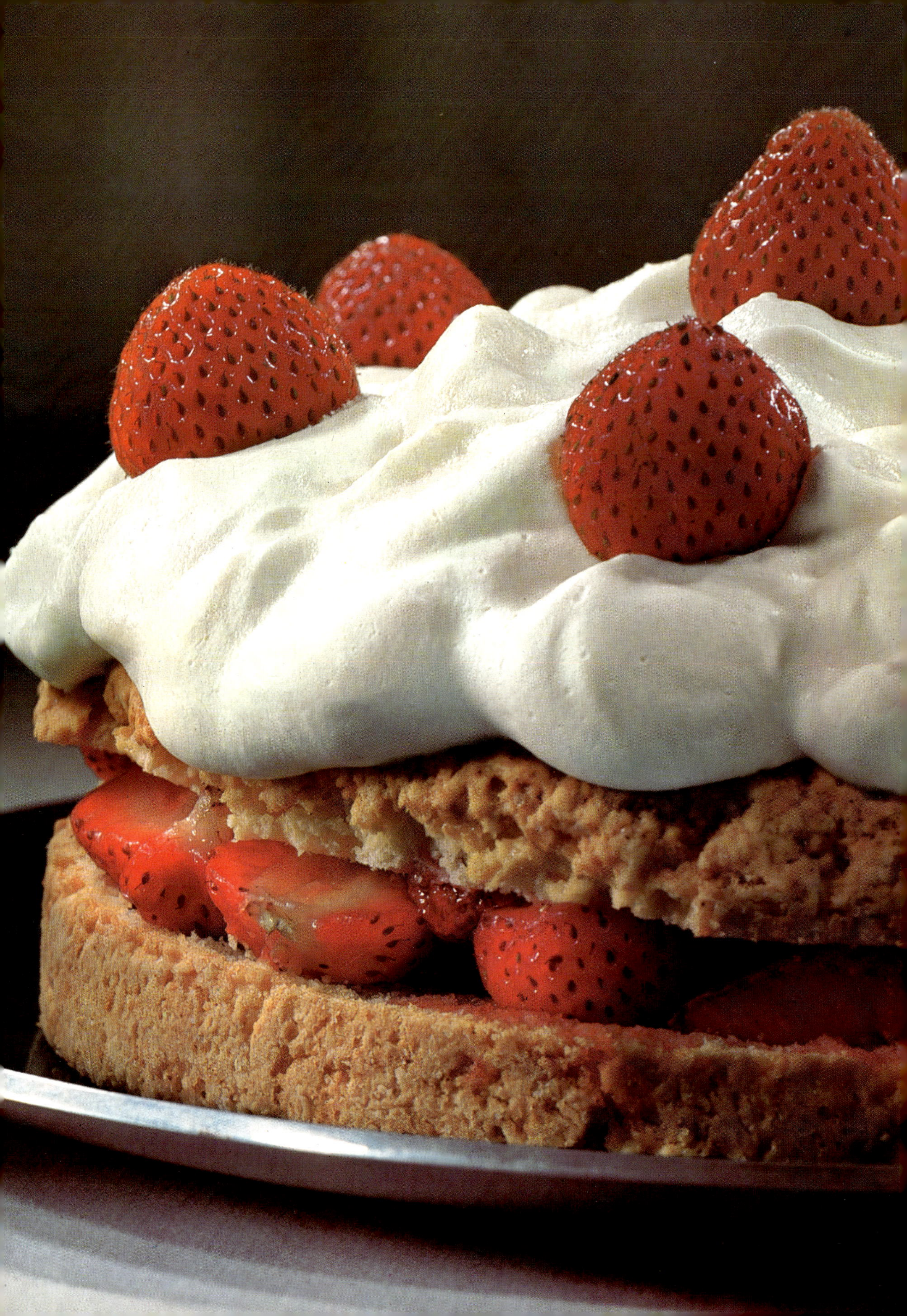

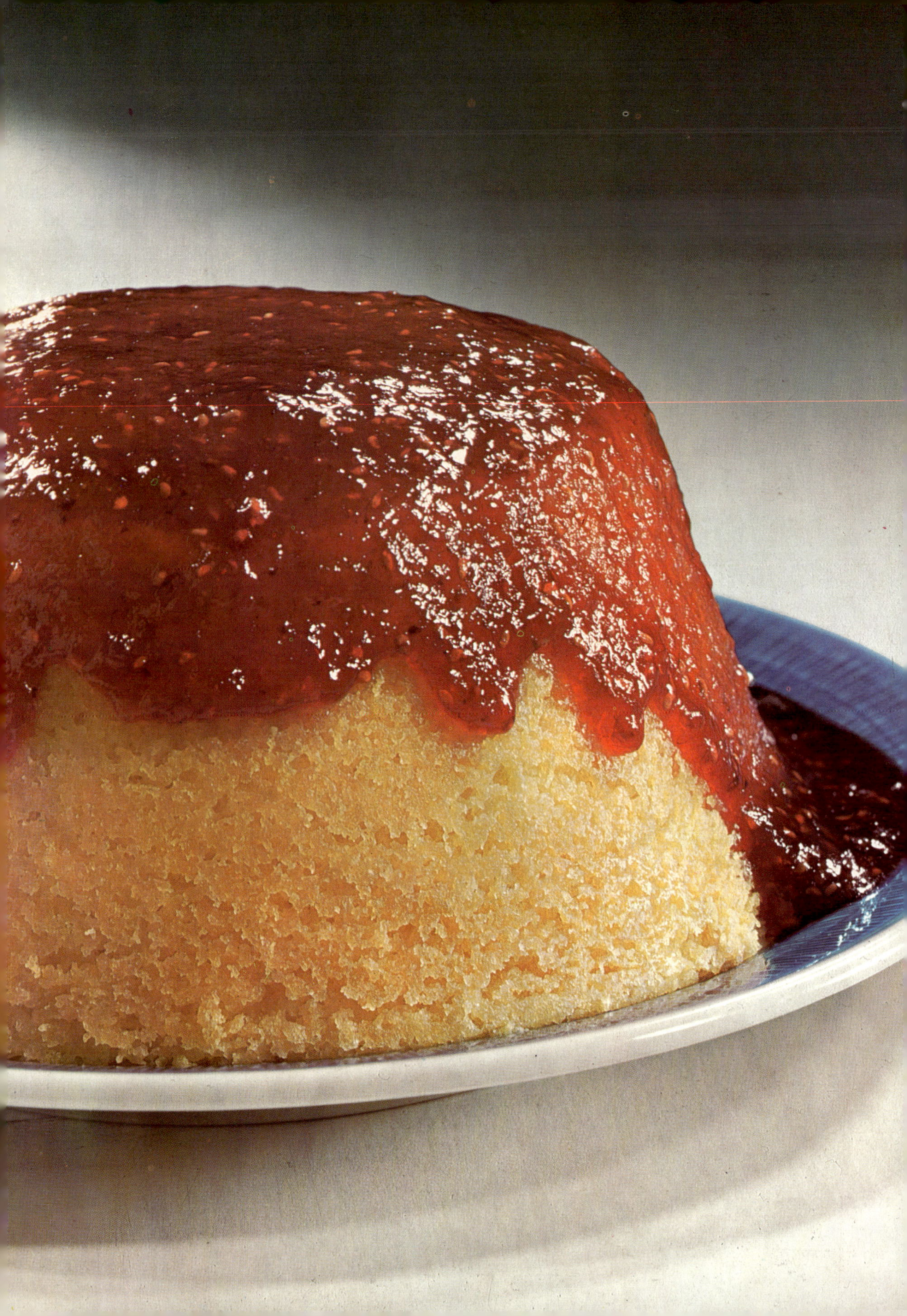

Lemon Cornflake Flan

1 pkt. lemon jelly
¾ pint water
1 small can of evaporated milk

For the Cornflake Crust
3 oz. cornflakes
1 tsp. ground cinnamon
2 oz. margarine
2 oz. sugar
1 tbsp. golden syrup
Grated chocolate (optional)

Grease a 7-inch flan tin or shallow pie plate. Dissolve the jelly in ¼ pint boiling water, add ½ pint cold water, mix well and leave in a cool place. Crush the cornflakes and mix with the cinnamon. Heat the margarine, sugar and golden syrup together, allow to boil for 1 minute, then stir in the cornflake mixture until all the flakes are well coated. Line the pie plate with this cornflake mixture, pressing it firmly against the sides to give a firm, smooth "crust". Leave in a cool place until firm. When the jelly is beginning to set, whisk it until frothy and then stir in the evaporated milk and whisk again until the mixture is light and fluffy. Pile into the crust and sprinkle with grated chocolate.

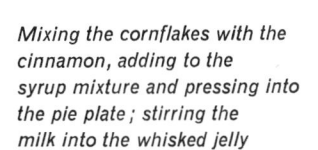

Mixing the cornflakes with the cinnamon, adding to the syrup mixture and pressing into the pie plate; stirring the milk into the whisked jelly

Steamed Jam Sponge: p 113

Cold Puddings

Layered Blancmange

A pkt. of banana blancmange
2 level tbsps. sugar
1 pint milk
2–3 level tbsps. cocoa powder

This page: making up the banana blancmange powder and layering the two mixtures. Opposite page: making Jam Sauce

Mix together half the banana blancmange powder, 1 tbsp. sugar and 1 tbsp. milk in a bowl and blend to a smooth paste. Add the cocoa powder and the remaining sugar to the rest of the banana blancmange powder and blend to a smooth paste with milk. Heat the remaining milk, pour half of it into the plain banana paste and mix together; return the mixture to a saucepan and bring gently to the boil, stirring all the time until it becomes thick and smooth. Turn it into a clean bowl and cover with wetted greaseproof paper to prevent a skin forming.

Pour the rest of the heated milk on to the chocolate paste and repeat as for the plain banana mixture. Layer the chocolate and the banana mixture into 4 glasses and leave to set.

An equally attractive variation is based on a packet of raspberry blancmange powder; make it up in the ordinary way and put alternate layers of blancmange and slightly warmed raspberry jam into the glasses.

Sweet Sauces

Custard Sauce

Custard powder
1 pint milk
1 oz. sugar
Vanilla essence

Take the amount of custard powder directed on the packet and blend with a little of the cold milk until it is really smooth. Heat the rest of the milk and when it is hot but not boiling, pour it on to the blended powder. Return the mixture to the saucepan and bring to the boil, stirring all the time. Add the sugar and a few drops of vanilla essence to taste. Stir well and serve hot or cold.

Sweet White Sauce

1½ level tbsps. cornflour
½ pint milk
2 level tbsps. sugar

Blend the cornflour with a little of the cold milk until it is smooth, then add the sugar. Bring the rest of the milk to the boil and pour on to the blended cornflour, stirring well. Return the mixture to the saucepan and bring to the boil, stirring all the time.

Variations:

1. Flavour with a strip of lemon or orange rind, adding this to the milk before it is boiled; strain the sauce before using
2. Add a pinch of mixed spice
3. Add 1 level tbsp. of a red-coloured jam
4. Add a little rum or brandy
5. Add a little coffee essence
6. Add 1 level tbsp. cocoa to give a chocolate sauce.

Rich Lemon or Orange Sauce

1 large lemon or orange
1–2 level tbsps. sugar
1 oz. butter
1 level tbsp. flour
¼ pint water
1–2 egg yolks

Wipe the lemon or orange, grate the rind and rub it into the sugar. Melt the butter in a saucepan and stir in the flour or cornflour, then add the water gradually and stir until boiling. Simmer slowly for 2–3 minutes and add the sugar and the strained fruit juice. Remove the pan from the heat and quickly stir in the egg yolk. Pour at once into a sauce boat and serve.

Jam Sauce

4 level tbsps. raspberry jam
¼ pint water
2 level tsps. cornflour

Heat the jam and water together. Blend the cornflour with a little cold water. Pour the heated jam on to the blended cornflour, return the mixture to the pan and bring to the boil, stirring all the time.
If you wish, sieve the sauce before using, to remove the jam pips.

Sweet Sauces

Rich Chocolate Sauce (top photographs): melting the chocolate and butter and adding the remaining ingredients

Brandy Butter (lower photographs): adding the brandy to the butter and sugar and piling the sauce in a dish

Syrup Sauce

2 tbsps. water   Juice of ½ a lemon
4 tbsps. golden syrup

Put all the ingredients into a small pan, stir well and boil together for a few minutes.

Marmalade Sauce

1 oz. sugar   ¼ pint water
4 tbsps. marmalade   Lemon juice

Boil the sugar, marmalade and water together till syrupy, then add a few drops of lemon juice and strain the sauce. Serve hot.

Rich Chocolate Sauce for Ice Cream

2 oz. plain chocolate   1 tbsp. milk
½ oz. butter   1 tsp. vanilla essence

Break up the chocolate into small pieces, add the butter and heat in a basin over hot water until they melt. Remove from the heat and stir in the milk and essence.

Brandy Butter

3 oz. butter   2–3 tsps. brandy
3 oz. caster sugar

Cream the butter until pale and soft. Beat in the sugar gradually, then add the brandy a few drops at a time, taking care not to allow the mixture to curdle. The finished sauce should be pale and frothy. Pile it into a small dish and leave to harden before serving with Christmas Pudding.

Rolls, Bread Scones

Quick Rolls

8 oz. plain flour
2 level tsp. baking powder
1 level tsp. salt
1 oz. butter or margarine
¼ pint milk

Heat the oven to hot (425°F., mark 7). Sieve the dry ingredients into a bowl. Rub in the fat until the mixture resembles fine breadcrumbs. Make a well in the centre, add the milk and mix together with a round-bladed knife. Draw it together with the finger-tips and turn it on to a lightly floured board. Divide into 9 portions and shape into round rolls. Place on a greased and floured baking sheet, brush with milk and bake towards the top of the oven for 15–20 minutes.

Eat these rolls while they are still fresh.

Rolls, Bread, Scones

Quick Wholemeal Loaves

3 level tsps. sugar
¾ pint water (approx.)
½ oz. dried yeast (1 level tbsp.)
12 oz. wholemeal flour
12 oz. white flour
3 level tsps. salt

Heat the oven to hot (425°F., mark 7). Grease 2 baking trays. Dissolve 1 tsp. of sugar in a cupful of warm water (taken from the measured amount), then sprinkle the dried yeast on the top; leave until frothy (10–15 minutes). Add with the rest of liquid to the dry ingredients and mix to a soft, scone-like dough. Divide the dough into 2 portions, shape into rounds and flatten the tops. Place on a baking tray, and put inside a greased polythene bag. Leave to rise until the dough is doubled in size and will spring back when lightly pressed with a floured finger. Bake in the centre of the oven for about 30 minutes, or until the loaves are firm to the touch and sound hollow when tapped underneath.

Adding the yeast liquid to the dry ingredients and putting the dough to rise

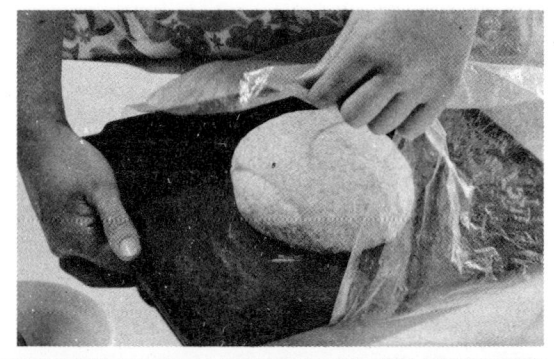

Scones

8 oz. self-raising flour
¼ level tsp. salt
1½ oz. butter or margarine
1 oz. sugar
2 oz. currants
¼ pint milk (approx.)

Heat the oven to hot (425°F., mark 7). Grease a baking tray. Sift the flour and salt into a bowl. Cut the fat into it and rub in until the mixture resembles fine breadcrumbs. Stir in the sugar and currants. Add the milk to give a fairly soft dough. Draw the mixture together with the tips of the fingers and turn on to a very lightly floured board; form into a flat round and roll out 1 inch thick. Cut out 2-inch rounds with a plain cutter and place on a greased baking tray. Brush the tops with milk and cook towards the top of the oven for about 10 minutes, until golden-brown. Remove to a cooling rack and leave till cold. Serve split in half and buttered.

Adding the milk, rolling out and cutting the dough, brushing with milk to glaze

Rolls, Bread, Scones

Drop Scones or Scotch Pancakes

4 oz. self-raising flour   1 egg
½–1 oz. sugar   ¼ pint milk

These scones may be cooked on a special "girdle", in a heavy frying pan or on a solid hot-plate. Season the surface by rubbing with salt on a pad of kitchen paper; wipe clean and grease the surface very lightly.

Put the flour and sugar in a bowl, break in the egg, add half the milk and beat until smooth. Add the rest of the milk and beat until bubbles rise to the surface. Heat the girdle, pan or hot-plate until the fat is hazing. Wipe the surface with a piece of kitchen paper, spoon on the batter and cook on one side. When bubbles appear on the surface of the scone, turn it over with a palette knife and cook for another ½–1 minute, or until golden-brown. Remove and place on a cooling rack. Cover with a clean tea cloth, while the rest are being cooked. Serve buttered.

Preparing a frying pan, mixing the batter and frying the scones

Cakes and Biscuits

Rock Buns

8 oz. self-raising flour
A pinch of salt
½ level tsp. mixed spice
½ level tsp. ground nutmeg
4 oz. butter or margarine
4 oz. dried fruit
1 oz. candied peel, chopped
4 oz. sugar
1 egg, beaten
Milk to mix

Heat the oven to fairly hot (375°F., mark 5). Grease a baking tray. Sift together the flour, salt and spices. Rub in the fat. Add the fruit, peel and sugar and mix well. Add the egg and enough milk to give a stiff dough. Spoon the mixture in small piles on to the greased tray and bake towards the top of the oven for 15–20 minutes.

As a variation, replace the dried fruit and peel by 4 oz. chopped stoned dates and ½ oz. chopped crystallised ginger.

Making the rock cake mixture and putting it on to the baking tray

Cakes and Biscuits

Jam Buns

8 oz. self-raising flour
A pinch of salt
3 oz. butter or margarine
3 oz. caster sugar
3–4 tbsps. milk
Jam
Milk to glaze

Heat the oven to fairly hot (375°F., mark 5). Grease a baking tray. Sift together the flour and salt, then rub in the fat. Add the sugar and mix all together thoroughly; add the milk to give a stiff dough. Turn out on to a floured board and form into a roll. Cut off pieces ¾ inch thick and place on the baking tray. Make a hollow in the centre of each and fill with jam. Brush round the edges with milk and bake for 15–20 minutes, until golden-brown.

Rubbing in fat, adding liquid, shaping buns and putting in the jam

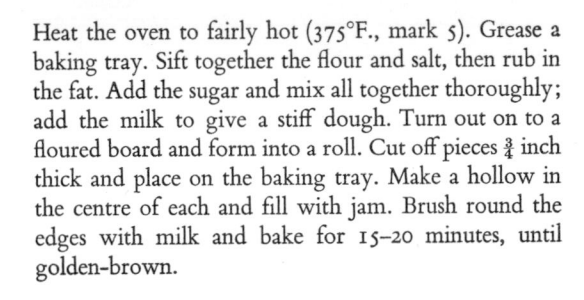

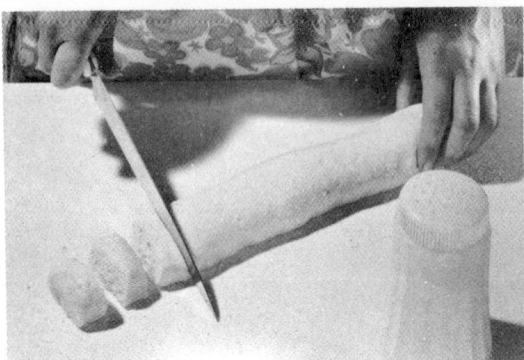

Queen Cakes

4 oz. margarine
4 oz. caster sugar
2 eggs, beaten
2 oz. sultanas
4 oz. self-raising flour, sifted
A little milk

Heat the oven to fairly hot (375°F., mark 5). Spread 12 paper cases out on a baking tray. Cream the margarine and sugar well until pale and fluffy, then add the eggs gradually, beating well after each addition. Add the fruit to the creamed mixture, then carefully fold in the flour. If necessary add a little milk to give a dropping consistency. Half-fill the paper cases with the mixture and bake near the top of the oven for 15–20 minutes, until golden.

Setting out the baking cases, making the mixture and filling the cases

Cakes and Biscuits

Almond Fingers

4 oz. plain flour
A pinch of salt
2 oz. butter
1 level tsp. caster sugar
1 egg, separated
Cold water to mix
4 oz. icing sugar, sifted
4 oz. almonds, blanched
   and chopped

Choose an oblong tin measuring about 10 by 5 inches. Heat the oven to moderate (350°F., mark 4). Sift the flour and salt into a basin and rub in the fat. Mix in the sugar, then add the egg yolk and sufficient cold water to mix to a firm dough. Turn on to a floured board and knead lightly. Use this pastry to line the tin. Whisk the egg white until stiff, then fold in the icing sugar. Spread this mixture over the pastry base and sprinkle the nuts evenly on top. Bake for about 30 minutes. When cold, cut into about 14 fingers.

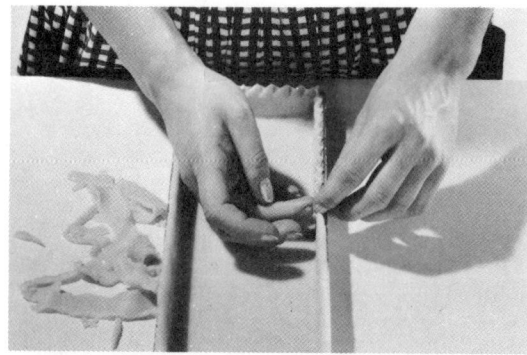

Decorating the pastry case, mixing and adding the filling and adding the topping

Coconut Tarts

4 oz. plain flour
A pinch of salt
2 oz. butter
1 level tsp. caster sugar for pastry
1 egg yolk and cold water to mix
Raspberry jam

2 oz. margarine
2 oz. caster sugar for filling
1 egg, beaten
2 oz. desiccated coconut
1 oz. self-raising flour, sifted

Heat the oven to fairly hot (375°F., mark 5). Prepare 16–18 patty tins. Sift the plain flour and salt into a basin, rub in the butter lightly and stir in the 1 tsp. sugar; add the egg yolk and enough water to mix to a firm dough. Turn on to a floured board and knead lightly, roll out and cut into rounds large enough to fit the patty tins. Line the tins with pastry and put a little jam in each.

Cream the margarine and 2 oz. sugar together, beat in the egg a little at a time, then fold in the coconut and self-raising flour and add a little water if necessary to give a soft dropping consistency. Place in spoonfuls in the lined patty tins and bake for 15–20 minutes, until golden and firm to the touch.

Lining the tins with pastry, adding jam, making and adding the coconut mixture

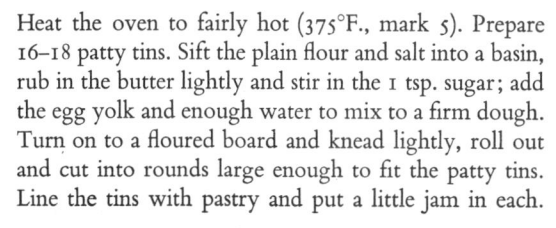

Cakes and Biscuits

Lining Cake Tins

Lining a Round Tin

Stand the tin on a sheet of greaseproof paper and draw round it with a pencil. Cut out the round of paper just inside the pencilled line. Measure the depth of the tin and add an extra 2 inches; now cut a strip of greaseproof paper this width and long enough to encircle the tin. (It may be necessary to cut 2 strips to give the right length.) Turn up ½ inch along one long edge of the strip and make slanting cuts at ½-inch intervals, going as far as the crease. Grease the inside of the tin and fit the strips neatly into place round the sides, with the snipped edge on the base. Fit the round of paper into the bottom. Finally, grease all the lining paper thoroughly.

Lining a Square Tin

Follow the general directions given for a round tin, taking special care to fit the paper right into the corners.
Notes: With a rich fruit cake, double greaseproof paper should be used to prevent overbrowning and drying of the outside crust. When cooking a Christmas cake wrap an extra layer of brown or newspaper round the outside of the tin.
If you notice that a cake is browning too quickly on top, place a piece of paper over it for the second half of the cooking time.
Siliconised papers need no greasing.
Siliconised tins of course need no lining, as they have been specially treated. To preserve the finish, avoid using sharp knives and harsh abrasives.

ROUND TIN

SQUARE TIN

Walnut Loaf Cake

10 oz. self-raising flour
1 level tsp. mixed spice
6 oz. brown sugar
2–3 oz. walnuts, chopped
2 eggs, beaten
¼ pint milk plus 3–4 tbsps. (if necessary)

Heat the oven to cool (325°F., mark 3). Grease and line a loaf tin measuring 9 by 5 inches approx. Sift the flour and spice and stir in the sugar and walnuts. Make a well in the centre and add the beaten eggs and ¼ pint milk, with a little extra milk if needed to give a stiff batter consistency. Pour into the prepared tin and bake just below the centre of the oven for 1½ hours. Cool, then store for 24 hours before cutting.

Adding liquid to the mixture and pouring it into the prepared tin

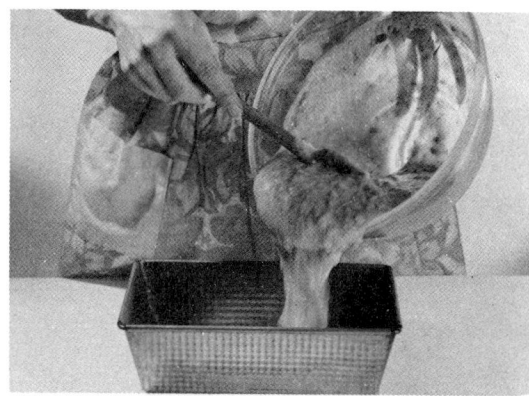

Cakes and Biscuits

Plain Fruit Cake

8 oz. self-raising flour
A pinch of salt
3 oz. margarine
3 oz. sugar
2 oz. currants
2 oz. sultanas
1 oz. candied peel, chopped
2 eggs, beaten
About 6 tbsps. milk to mix

Heat the oven to moderate (350°F., mark 4). Grease and line a 7-inch round cake tin. Sift the flour and salt and rub in the fat. Add the sugar, fruit and peel, then add the eggs and enough milk to give a dropping consistency. Put into the tin, smoothing the top with a knife, and bake in the centre of the oven for about 1 hour, until the cake is golden-brown and firm to the touch. Turn out and cool on a rack.

Adding liquid to give a mixture of dropping consistency, putting into cake tin and turning out the cooked cake

Apricot Amber: p 98

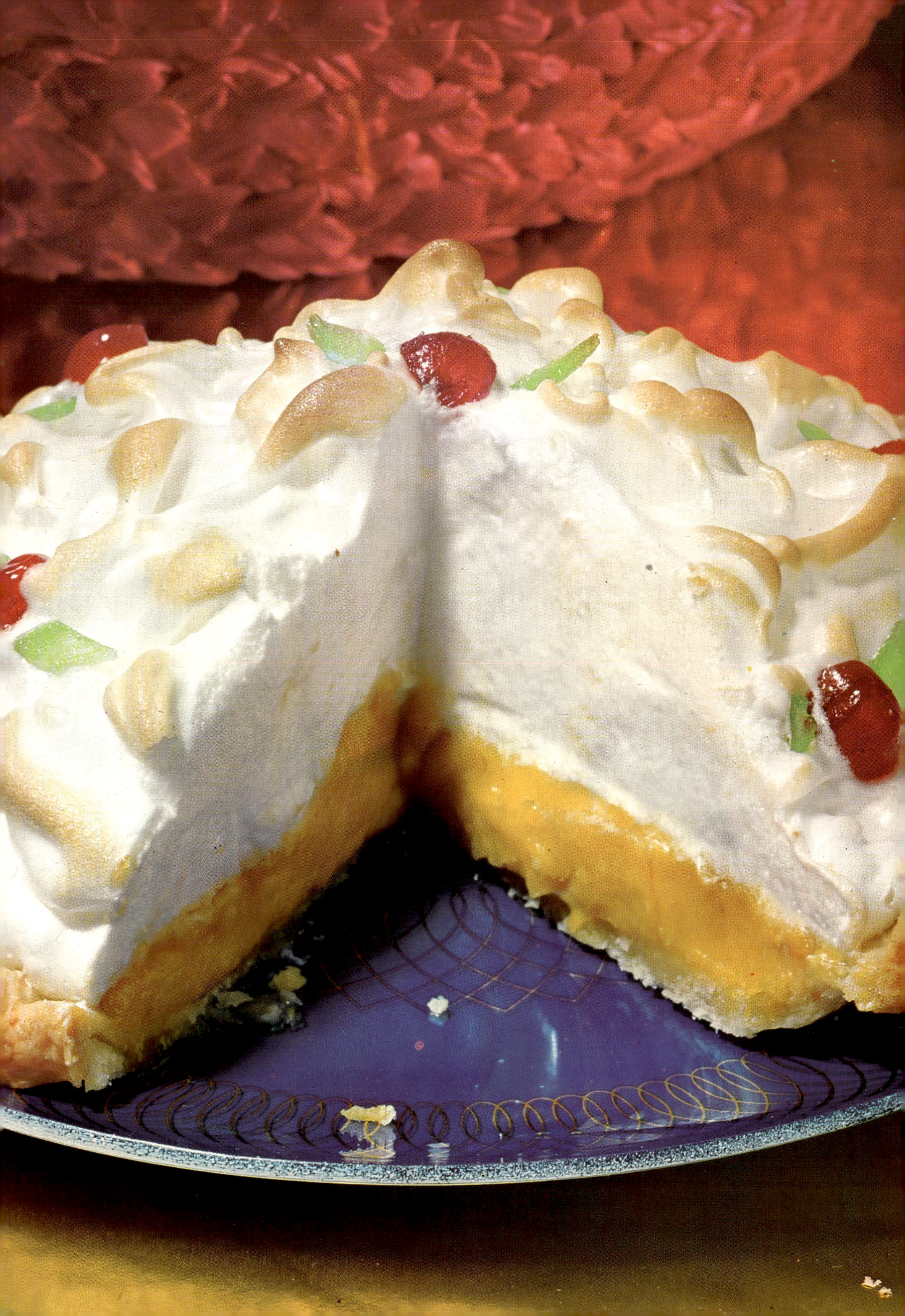

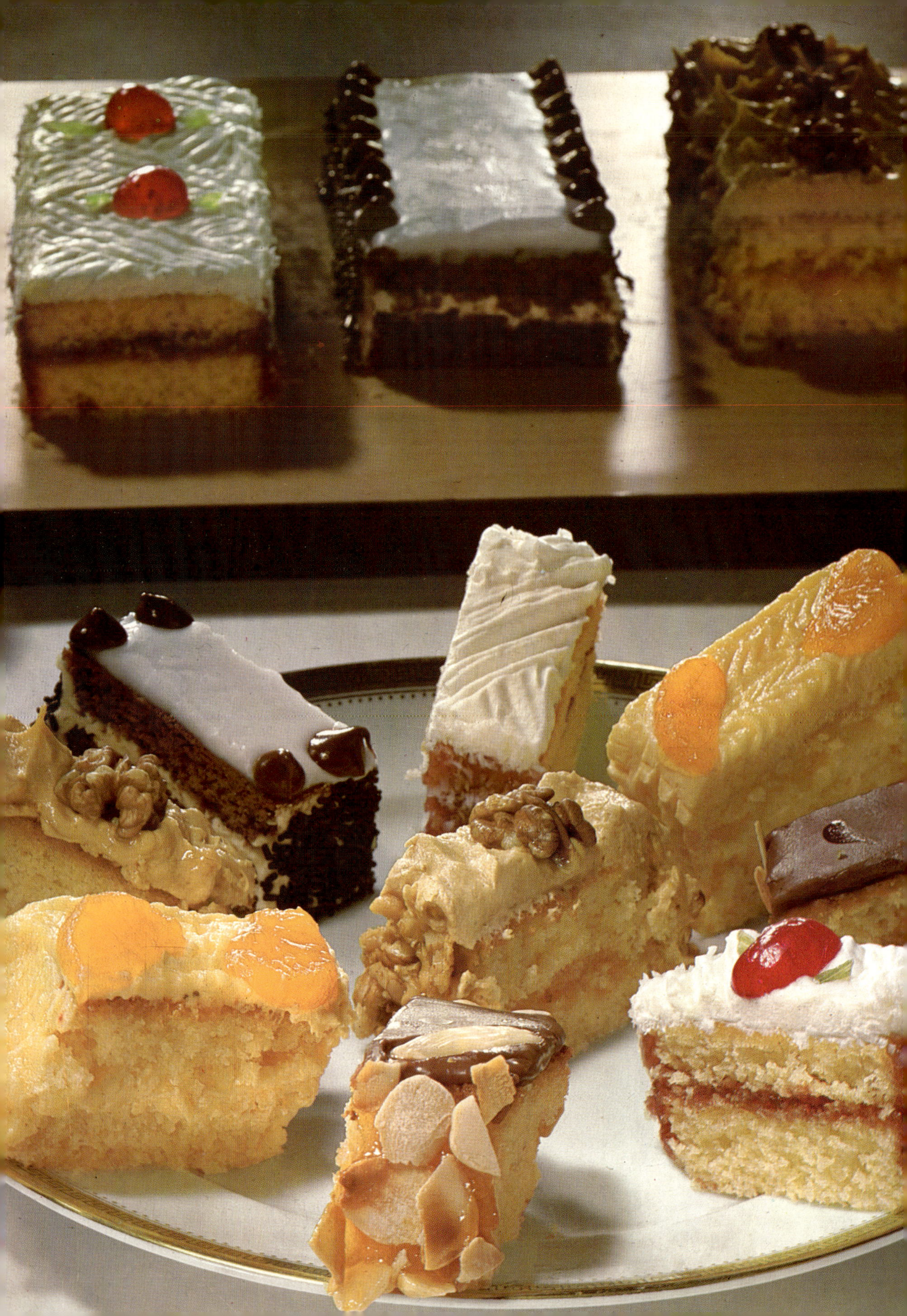

Apple Cake

8 oz. self-raising flour
½ level tsp. cinnamon
4 oz. butter or
   margarine
4 oz. soft brown sugar

2 eggs, beaten
2 oz. raisins, stoned
   or seedless
2 cooking apples,
   stewed and pulped

Heat the oven to cool (325°F., mark 3). Grease and line a loaf tin measuring 9 by 5 inches approx. Sift together the flour and cinnamon. Cream together the fat and sugar until light and fluffy. Gradually add the beaten eggs. Fold in half of the sifted flour. Add the raisins and apple pulp and the remaining flour and fold in. Turn the mixture into the prepared tin and bake just below the centre of the oven for about 1½ hours. Turn out, cool and serve cut in slices and buttered.

Sifting in half the flour and adding the raisins and apple pulp

Cakes and Biscuits

Cherry Cake

6 oz. butter
6 oz. caster sugar
2 eggs, beaten
8 oz. self-raising
  flour
A pinch of salt
4–6 oz. glacé cherries,
  quartered
Vanilla essence
Milk if required

Heat the oven to warm (325°F., mark 3). Grease a loaf tin measuring 9 by 5 inches approx. and line with greased greaseproof paper. Cream the butter and sugar, then gradually beat in the eggs. Sift together the flour and salt and add the cherries. Fold this mixture into the creamed mixture and add a few drops of essence and enough milk to give a dropping consistency. Put into the prepared tin and bake for $1\frac{1}{4}$–$1\frac{1}{2}$ hours, until firm to touch and golden in colour.

Cherry Cake

Ginger Loaf Cake

4 oz. butter
2 oz. sugar
2 tbsps. golden syrup
2 eggs, beaten
8 oz. self-raising
  flour
2–3 level tsps. ground
  ginger

Heat the oven to warm (325°F., mark 3). Grease a loaf tin and line with greased greaseproof paper. Cream together the butter, sugar and syrup, then gradually beat in the eggs. Sift together the flour and ginger, then fold into the creamed mixture. Put into the prepared tin and bake in the centre of the oven for $1\frac{1}{4}$ hours, until golden and firm to the touch. Cool on a rack.

For a more festive effect, cover the top of the cake with glacé icing when it is cold; decorate with pieces of crystallised ginger.

Ginger Loaf

Walnut Cake

4 oz. shelled walnuts
5 oz. butter
5 oz. caster sugar
3 eggs, beaten
8 oz. self-raising flour
A pinch of salt
Grated rind of 1 lemon

Heat oven to warm (325°F., mark 3). Grease and line a 7-inch tin. Keep a few walnuts whole to decorate and chop the rest coarsely. Cream butter and sugar and beat in egg gradually. Sift flour and salt and mix with lemon rind and chopped nuts. Fold into the creamed mixture and mix well. Put into the tin, place the whole nuts on top and bake for 1¼–1½ hours.

Rich Fruit Cake

8 oz. each currants, sultanas and raisins
4 oz. glacé cherries
4 oz. candied peel, chopped
3 oz. blanched almonds
8 oz. butter
8 oz. moist brown sugar
4 eggs, beaten
1 tbsp. black treacle (optional)
8 oz. plain flour
A pinch of salt
Milk if required

Walnut Cake

Heat oven to warm (325°F., mark 3). Grease and line an 8-inch tin. Prepare fruit and chop cherries, peel and nuts. Cream fat and sugar and beat in eggs gradually, with treacle if used. Sift flour and salt and mix with fruit. Fold into the creamed mixture and add enough milk to give a dropping consistency. Put into the prepared tin and bake towards the bottom of the oven for 2 hours. Reduce oven heat to cool (300°F., mark 2) and bake for a further 1½–2 hours.

This mixture can be used for a birthday cake—see pages 152–157 for icing and decorating.

Rich Fruit Cake

Cakes and Biscuits

Victoria Sandwich Cake

4 oz. butter
4 oz. caster sugar
2 eggs, beaten
4 oz. self-raising flour, sifted
1–2 rounded tbsps. jam
Caster sugar to dredge

Heat the oven to fairly hot (375°F., mark 5). Grease two 7-inch sandwich cake tins; cut a round of greaseproof paper to put in the base of each.
Cream the fat and sugar until pale and fluffy. Beat the eggs in a little at a time, beating well after each addition. Lightly fold in half the flour, using a tablespoon, then fold in the rest. Place half the mixture in each tin and level it with a knife. Bake both cakes on the same shelf, just above the oven centre, for about 20 minutes, or until they are well risen, golden, firm to the touch and beginning to shrink away from the sides of the tins. When cool, sandwich together with jam and sprinkle the top with caster sugar.

Variations:
This mixture may be varied in many ways.

Chocolate—replace 1 oz. of the flour with 1 oz. chocolate powder. Sandwich the cakes together with vanilla or chocolate butter cream.

Orange or Lemon—add 2 level tsps. orange or lemon rind to the mixture. Sandwich the cakes together with orange or lemon curd or orange or lemon butter cream. Use the juice of the fruit to make glacé icing for the top.

Coffee—include 2 tsps. instant coffee or 1 tbsp. strong black coffee to the creamed mixture, adding it with the egg.

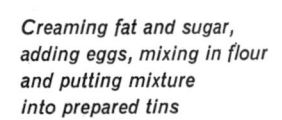

Creaming fat and sugar, adding eggs, mixing in flour and putting mixture into prepared tins

Gingerbread

8 oz. plain flour
2–3 level tsps. ground ginger
2 level tsps. baking powder
½ level tsp. bicarbonate of soda
½ level tsp. salt
6 tbsps. syrup
1 tbsp. black treacle (optional)
3 oz. margarine
4 oz. soft brown sugar
1 egg, beaten
⅛–¼ pint milk

Heat the oven to warm (325°F., mark 3). Grease and line an 8-inch square tin.

Sift the dry ingredients together. Warm the syrup, treacle (if used), fat and sugar. Make a well in the centre of the dry ingredients and add the syrup mixture. Add the egg and some of the milk, and stir well; add more milk if necessary to give a pouring consistency. Pour the mixture into the tin and bake for about 1 hour, until firm to the touch. When the gingerbread is cool, remove the paper and cut into squares.

Warming the syrup, fat, etc., adding to the dry ingredients and pouring the mixture into the lined tin

Cakes and Biscuits

Christmas Cake

1 lb. 2 oz. currants
8 oz. sultanas
8 oz. stoned raisins
6 oz. glacé cherries
4 oz. candied peel
10 oz. plain flour
A pinch of salt
½ level tsp. ground cinnamon
½ level tsp. mixed spice
Grated rind of ½ a lemon
10 oz. butter
10 oz. soft brown sugar
1 tbsp. black treacle
6 eggs, beaten
3 tbsps. brandy

Heat the oven to cool (300°F., mark 1–2). Grease and line a 9-inch cake tin and tie a band of brown paper round the outside.

Clean the fruit a day in advance. Halve the cherries and chop the peel. Sift together the flour, salt and spices and add the fruit, mixing well, then add the lemon rind. Cream the butter and sugar until light and fluffy. Add the black treacle to the eggs and beat this mixture gradually into the creamed mixture. Fold in the flour and fruit, then the brandy. Bake near the bottom of the oven for about 4½ hours. To avoid over-browning, cover the top with several thicknesses of paper after 2½ hours.

For a richer flavour, prick the cooked cake with a fine skewer and slowly pour 2–3 tbsps. of brandy over it before storing.

Store it wrapped in greaseproof paper in an airtight tin; failing a suitable tin, wrap the cake lightly in aluminium foil.

Cover with almond paste and royal icing and decorate as liked—see next page for icing recipes and the method of carrying out the decorations shown opposite.

Combining the dry ingredients and fruit, creaming the fat and sugar, adding the treacle and eggs and putting the mixture into the tin

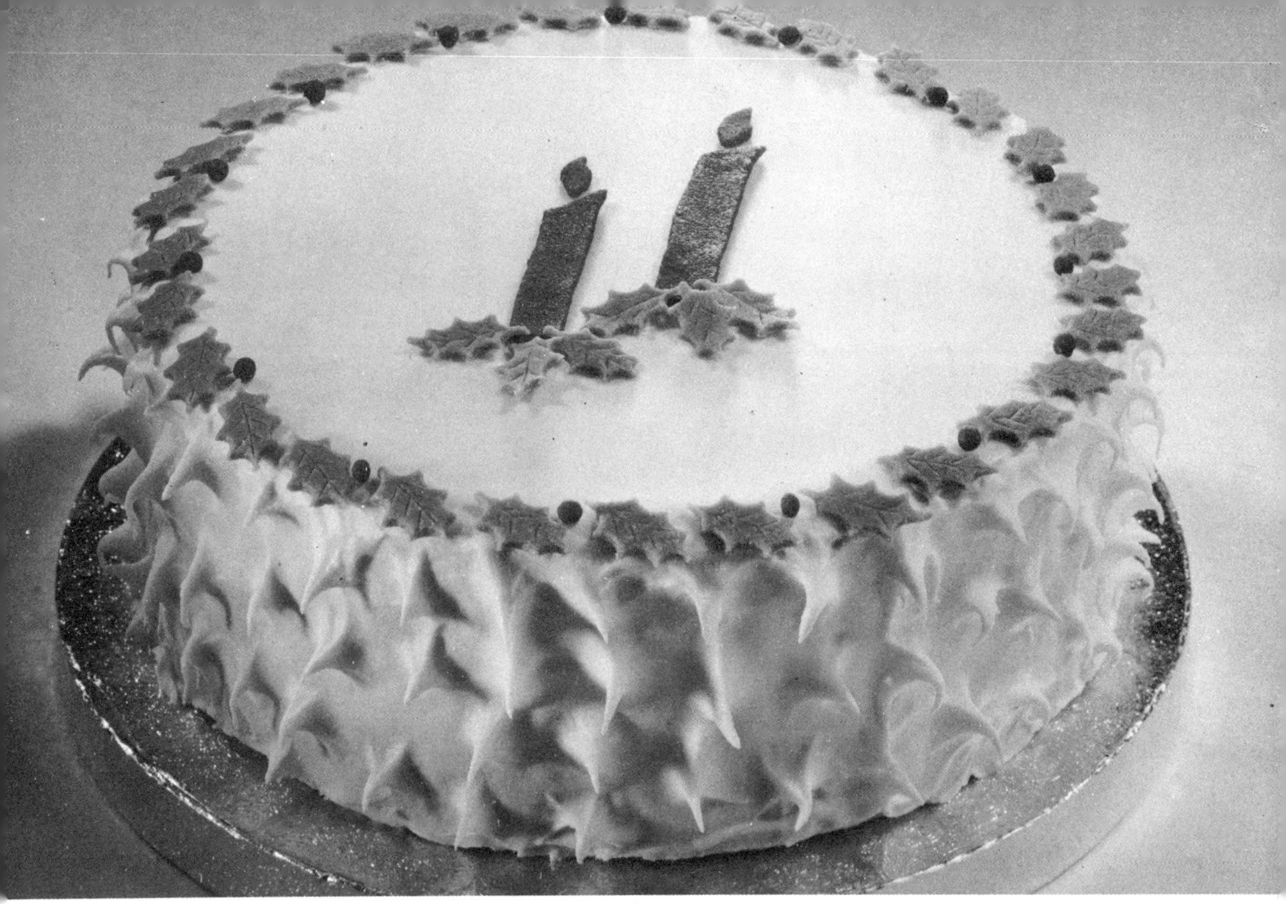

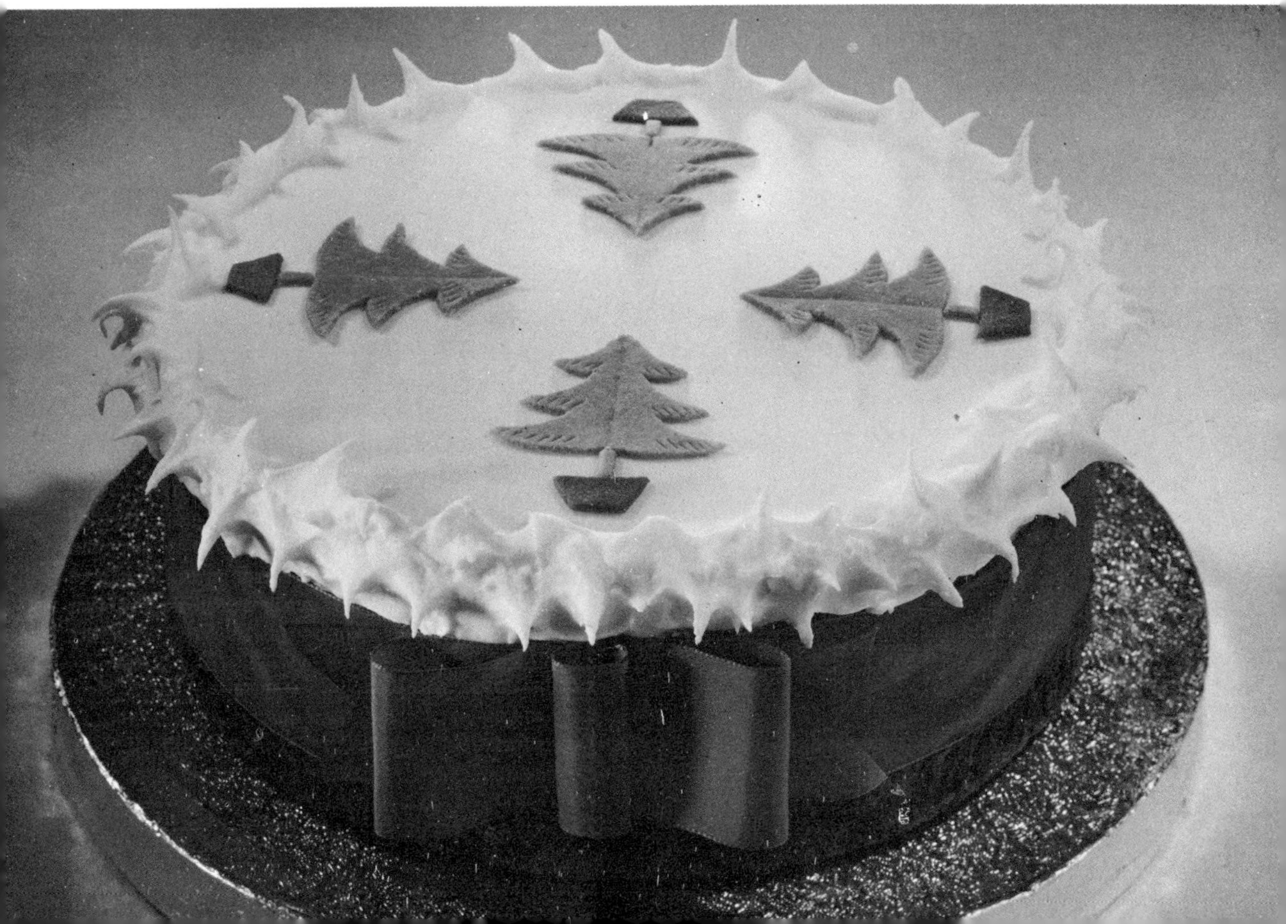

Cakes and Biscuits

Icing and Decorating a Christmas Cake

Almond Paste

12 oz. icing sugar
12 oz. ground almonds
1 beaten egg
1 tsp. almond essence
The juice of ½ a lemon

Sift the sugar and stir in the almonds. Add the beaten egg and almond essence and gradually stir in the dry ingredients, adding enough of the lemon juice to form a stiff dough. Form into a ball and knead lightly to remove

Putting paste round sides of cake, placing cake on round of paste that will form the top, neatening edges and turning cake right way up

any cracks. This amount is sufficient to cover top and sides of a 9-inch cake. If you intend to decorate the top only of the cake, make up half the amount. Cut off and reserve a small piece if you want to make almond paste decorations.

To Almond-ice the Cake

Trim the top of the cake to make it completely level. Measure round it, using a piece of string. Sieve ½ lb. apricot jam and brush it generously round the sides of the cake.

Cut the almond paste in half. Halve one portion again and form each quarter-portion into a sausage-shape; roll out each of these half as long as the piece of string and as wide as the cake is deep. Press the strips firmly on to the sides of the cake, smooth the joins with a knife and square the edges. Roll the cake edgewise on the table or board to get a flat finish. Brush the top of the cake and the top edge of the almond paste with jam. Dredge the table top or board heavily with icing sugar, then roll out the remaining paste to a round to fit the top of the cake. Put the cake upside-down, exactly in the centre of the almond paste, press down firmly and smooth the join. Turn the cake the right way up and leave for at least 24 hours before icing—preferably for 6–7 days.

Almond Paste Decorations

Decorations for a Christmas cake can be made very easily from almond paste. Choose a design with a simple, fairly bold outline—stars, candles, Christmas trees, holly leaves—draw it on stiff paper and cut out the pattern. Some parts of the design may look more attractive if carried out in a second colour, e.g., the tub of a Christmas tree or the flame of a candle, but do not use more than two colours, or the design will look too fussy. Cut off the portion of the paper pattern that is to be made in the second colour.

Add a little edible colouring to a piece of the almond paste, kneading it in until the colour is even. Sprinkle the working surface with a little icing sugar and roll out the almond paste very thinly. Put on it the pattern pieces that are to be made in that particular colour and cut round them with a sharp-pointed knife. (Do not press too firmly on the almond paste or finger marks will show.) Remove the patterns, neaten up the edges of the paste pieces if necessary and use the pointed knife to mark in any veins, branches, etc. Cut out the remaining shapes from a piece of almond paste tinted with the second colour. For holly berries make tiny balls of red paste. Leave the shapes on a plate until quite dry—2–3 days if possible—or they will mark the royal icing. Lay any leaves over a twist of greaseproof paper to give them a life-like curve.

Draw a circle on a piece of paper the size of the cake top and arrange the almond paste pieces on it in the chosen pattern. Then, using a pair of tweezers, lift each piece into the same position on the cake top and stick it with a tiny spot of icing.

A birthday cake may be decorated in a similar way; for a child, use nursery rhyme or toy cut-outs.

Royal Icing

2 lb. icing sugar   2 tsps. glycerine
4 egg whites

Use completely fresh icing sugar that is quite free from lumps. Stir the egg whites in a bowl until they are broken up but not bubbly. Gradually add the sugar until the mixture is of a thick coating consistency. Add the glycerine and stir for 20 minutes (do not beat or bubbles will form), until the icing is smooth, white and stiff enough for peaks to be easily formed on the surface when it is "pulled" up with a spoon. Remove 1 tbsp. of the icing, mix to a coating consistency with water, return it to the rest and mix until smooth.

This amount is sufficient to coat the top and sides of a 9-inch cake. To ice the top only, use half the quantities.

To Ice the Cake

Using a little icing, stick the cake firmly in the centre of an 11-inch cake board. Spoon half the icing on top of the cake; working the icing backwards and forwards with a knife to break any air bubbles, spread it over the top of the cake. Draw a clean ruler or a long palette knife across the top of the cake evenly and steadily, until the surface is smooth. Remove any extra icing that has been pushed to the edges. Work the rest of the icing around the sides of the cake in the same way.

Before the icing starts to set, quickly draw it up into peaks round the sides and in a 1-inch border round the top of the cake, using a round-bladed knife. Allow the icing to harden for at least a day before adding any decorations.

If you are icing the top only, take the icing far enough down the sides to cover the almond icing completely. Rough up a 1-inch wide border round the top and the covered part of the sides. When the icing is set, tie a ribbon round the uncovered part of the sides.

Smoothing first top then sides of royal-iced cake

Cakes and Biscuits

Butter Cream

4 oz. icing sugar
2 oz. butter or margarine
Milk if required
A few drops of vanilla essence

Sift the sugar; place it with the butter in a basin and cream together with a wooden spoon until smooth, pale and of a creamy consistency—add a little milk if necessary. Beat in the vanilla essence.

Flavour the cream in any of the following ways:

Chocolate—include 1 level tbsp. sifted cocoa or 1 oz. melted and cooled chocolate.

Coffee—add 2 level tsps. instant coffee dissolved in 1 tsp. water.

Mocha—add 2–3 level tsps. sifted cocoa and 1 tsp. instant coffee.

Sifting the icing sugar, using butter cream as a filling and round the sides of a cake and marking a simple pattern

Orange or Lemon—add the grated rind of 1 orange or lemon.

Walnut—add 1–2 oz. chopped walnuts and a little vanilla essence.

Using Butter Cream
The amounts given make enough cream for one layer inside or on top of the cake. If the cake is to be both decorated all over and filled with butter cream, you will require double the quantities.

As a Filling—spread the cream evenly over the lower half of the cake, taking it right to the edges, then put the top half of the cake neatly in place.

To Cover the Cake—spread the butter cream evenly all over the sides, then on the top of the cake. The sides may be rolled in chopped nuts or chocolate vermicelli. To give a more interesting effect, the surface of the butter cream can be patterned by using a fork or knife (see the pictures on these pages) before being decorated with crystallised fruits, nuts, glacé cherries, angelica or chocolate drops.

Another variation is to coat the sides only with butter cream and use glacé icing on the top of the cake—see page 156.

155

Cakes and Biscuits

Glacé Icing

8 oz. icing sugar, sifted　　　Warm water to mix

Place the sugar in a basin and add the water very gradually until the icing is smooth and thick enough to coat the back of the spoon.

This basic icing may be varied as follows:

Orange or Lemon—replace the water by orange or lemon juice.

Chocolate—sift 1 level tbsp. cocoa with the icing sugar.

Coffee—dissolve 2 level tsps. instant coffee in 1 tsp. of the water and add this when mixing the icing.

Coloured—use edible bottled colourings to tint the icing—only a few drops are needed and they should be added when the icing is made.

Mixing the icing, rolling sides of cake in chopped nuts, icing the top and adding the decoration

Icing a Cake
The amounts given will make enough icing to cover a 7-inch cake.

The Sides of the Cake may be left plain or iced (in which case you will need a double quantity of icing). Alternatively, they may be brushed with melted jam and then rolled in chopped walnuts, chopped blanched almonds or lightly browned coconut. Any icing or decoration on the sides of the cake must be done before the top is iced.

To Ice the Top—Prepare any decorations which are to be used (such as nuts, cherries, angelica, chocolate drops, crystallised fruit or silver balls, candies).

Place the prepared cake on the plate on which it is to be served. Pour the icing on to the centre of the cake and spread it out evenly, stopping just inside the actual edges, to prevent the icing from dripping down the sides. Quickly put the decorations in place before the icing sets (see pictures opposite)—this holds them firmly and prevents the icing from cracking as it would do if they were added later.

The cake in the lower picture has the sides coated with butter cream, which is "roughed up" with a knife.

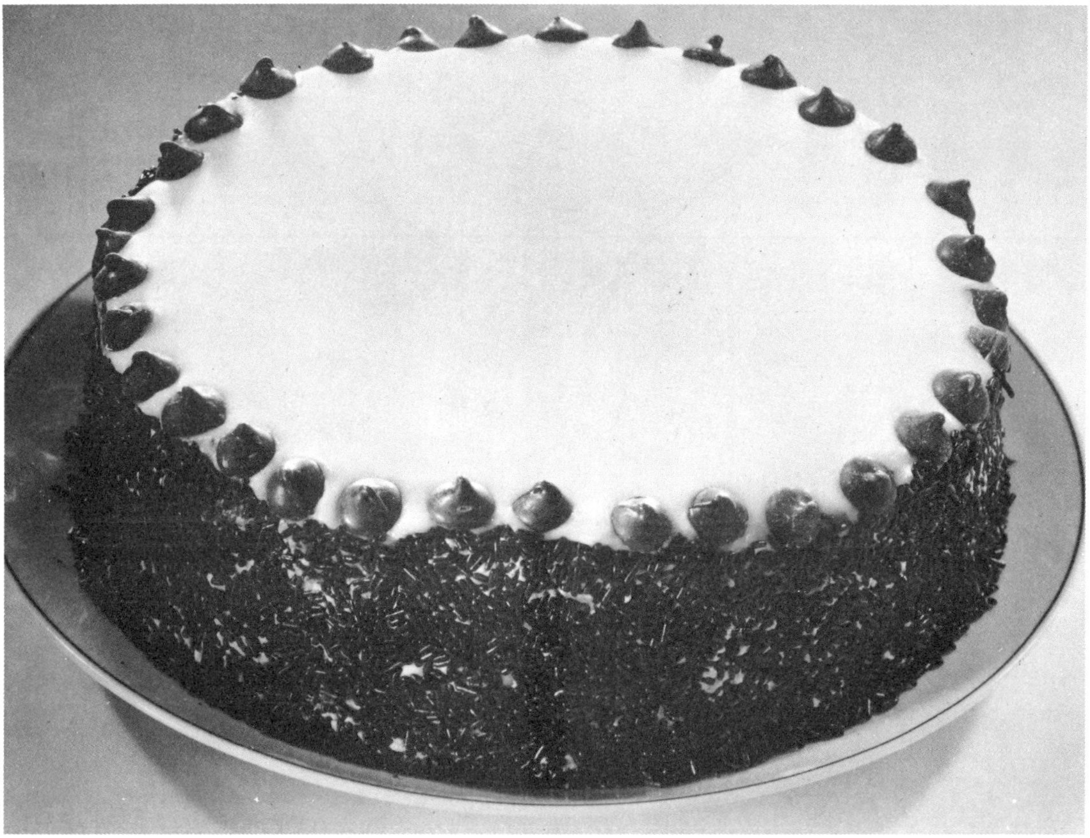

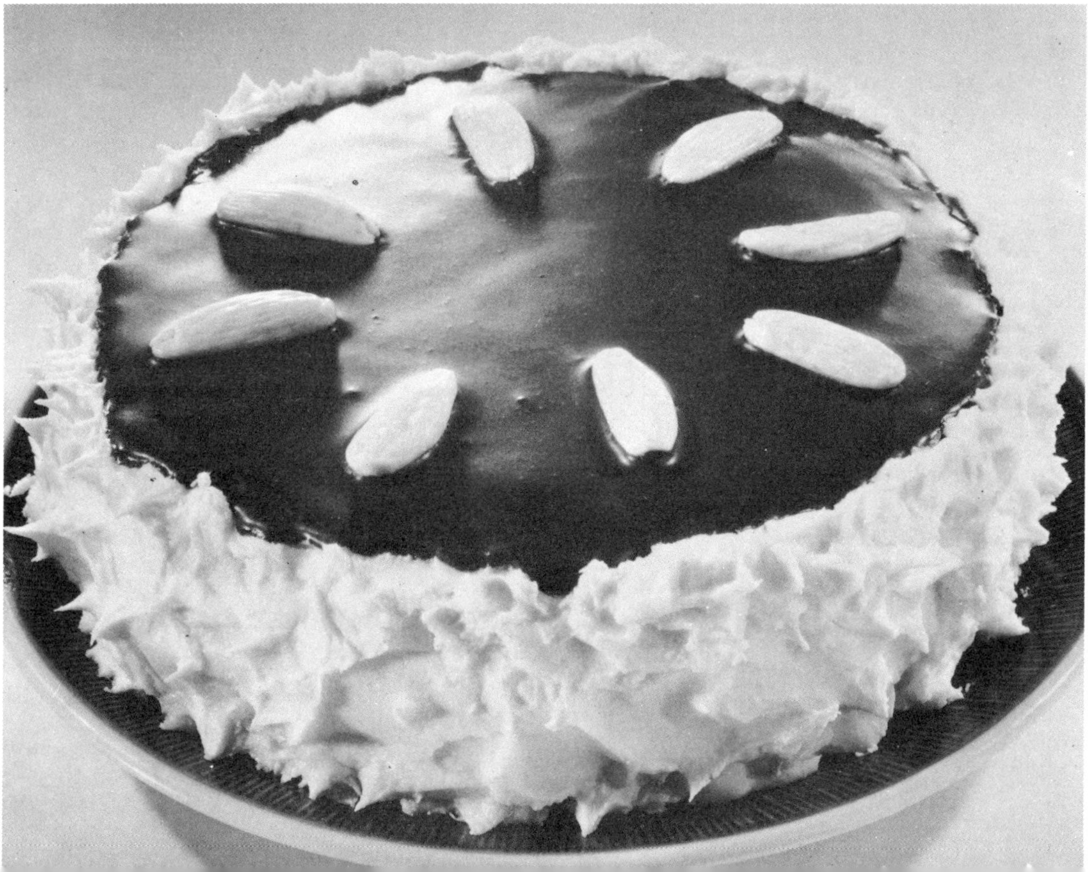

Cakes and Biscuits

Iced and Decorated Small Cakes

Fairy Cake Mixture

2 oz. butter or margarine
2 oz. caster sugar
1 egg, beaten
3 oz. self-raising flour, sifted
A little milk, if necessary

Heat the oven to fairly hot (375°F., mark 5). Cream the fat and sugar until pale, soft and fluffy. Beat in the egg gradually, then fold in the flour with a metal spoon, adding a little milk if necessary to give a dropping consistency. Place 10–12 paper cases on a baking sheet and half-fill with the mixture; bake the cakes near the top of the oven for about 15–20 minutes, until golden-brown and firm to the touch.

This basic mixture may be varied in a number of ways and decorated accordingly.

Chocolate—sift 1–2 level tbsps. cocoa with the flour.

Coffee—dissolve 2 level tsps. instant coffee in 1 tsp. hot water and add to the creamed mixture.

Mocha—sift 2 level tsps. cocoa and 1 level tsp. instant coffee with the flour.

Orange or Lemon—add the grated orange or lemon rind to the creamed mixture.

Decorating with Glacé Icing
When the cakes are cool, make glacé icing with 4 oz. sugar (see page 156), adding colouring and flavouring as wished. Place 1 tsp. icing in the centre of each cake and quickly add any decoration before the icing sets.
Alternatively coat the top of the cakes completely with the icing, easing it right up to the paper case with a small pointed knife. The cakes can then be decorated with a piece of glacé cherry, a halved walnut or almond, or sprinkled with grated chocolate, chocolate vermicelli, hundreds and thousands, desiccated coconut, chopped walnuts or toasted flaked almonds.

Decorating with Butter Cream or Cream
When the cakes are cool, cut a round piece from the centre of each, using a small pointed knife; this piece can then be cut in half to form "wings". Make up some butter cream (see page 154), using 4 oz. icing sugar and 2 oz. butter, and place a little in the centre of each cake, roughing it up with a knife or fork. Put on the two "wings", sticking them into the butter cream at an angle. If preferred, the round piece cut from the cakes may be left whole and stuck into the butter cream either straight or at an angle.
Another variation is to put 1 small tsp. jam in the centre of each cake before adding the butter cream.
Whipped fresh cream may be used instead of butter cream in any of these versions.

Quick Iced Cakes

This is a speedy method of producing a batch of small fancy cakes. Make up double the amount of Fairy Cake mixture given above, half-fill a shallow oblong cake tin and bake in a moderate oven (350°F., mark 4) for 35–40 minutes. When the cake is cool, ice and decorate, then cut into neat pieces. Alternatively, fill with butter cream or jam before cutting up and decorating.
Either glacé icing or butter cream may be used to coat the cake; butter cream may be marked with a fork or knife, as seen on pages 154–155. Add any decorations you like, such as halved or flaked nuts, chocolate drops, small sweets, silver or coloured balls, halved glacé cherries, with "leaves" of angelica, or pieces of canned or crystallised fruit. Arrange them so that when the cake is cut up, each piece will have its own well-placed decoration—see the colour picture facing page 145.

The top two pictures show cakes being decorated with glacé icing and cherries; the second pair show "butterfly" cakes filled with butter cream

159

Cakes and Biscuits

Shortbread

6 oz. plain flour
A pinch of salt
4 oz. butter
2 oz. caster sugar

Heat the oven to warm (325°F., mark 3). Grease a baking tray. Sift the flour and salt together, then rub in the butter until the mixture resembles fine breadcrumbs. Add the sugar, then knead the mixture until it binds well together. Turn this dough on to a lightly floured board and press into a round shape. Roll out to ½ inch thick, still keeping the round shape. Crimp the edges with the finger and thumb, mark the round into 8 sections with a knife and prick the surface with a fork. Bake towards the bottom of the oven for about 45 minutes, until firm and lightly coloured. Divide when cool.

Rubbing in the butter, kneading and rolling out the mixture and shaping the edge of the shortbread

Jammy Rings

3 oz. butter or margarine
3 oz. caster sugar
1 egg, beaten
Vanilla essence
6 oz. plain flour

Heat the oven to fairly hot (375°F., mark 5). Cream together the fat and sugar until light and fluffy. Add the egg and a few drops of vanilla essence, stir in the flour. Turn on to a board, knead very lightly and roll out to $\frac{1}{8}$ inch thick. Cut out rounds with a 2-inch plain cutter. Cut out the centre of half the rounds with a 1-inch plain cutter. Place on a baking sheet and bake in the centre of the oven for 10–15 minutes or till pale golden in colour. Place on a cooling rack. When the biscuits are cold, dust the rings very lightly with icing sugar and spread apricot, raspberry or greengage jam on the rounds; sandwich the rings and rounds together.

Forking in the flour, rolling out and cutting the dough and dredging the cooked rings with sugar

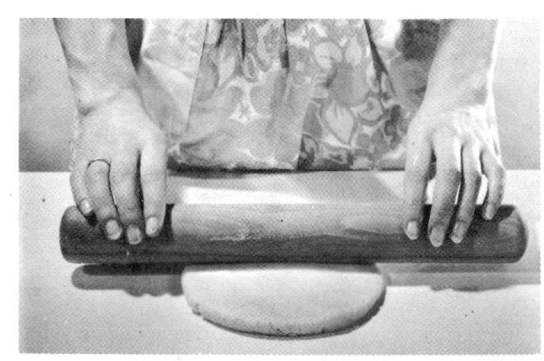

Cakes and Biscuits

Syrup Flapjacks

4 oz. butter   8 oz. rolled oats
1 oz. sugar   ½ level tsp. salt
2 tbsps. syrup, warmed

Heat the oven to moderate (350°F., mark 4). Grease a tin measuring about 8 by 10 inches.

Beat the butter and sugar until the mixture is creamy, then stir in the warmed syrup. Mix well, then work in the rolled oats and salt. Put the mixture into the tin and bake until brown. When it is firm, cut into pieces, but leave these in the tin until they are quite cold, or they may break up.

Stirring in the warmed syrup, adding the rolled oats, putting the mixture into the tin and cutting up

Gingerbread Men

4 oz. butter or margarine
4 oz. sugar
10 oz. plain flour
1 level tsp. bicarbonate of soda
3 level tsps. ground ginger
Warmed syrup (2½ tbsps.) approx.
A few currants

Heat the oven to moderate (350°F., mark 4). Grease a baking tray. Cream the fat and sugar until very soft. Sift the dry ingredients together, then work into the creamed mixture. Add the syrup to make a dough. Knead and roll out on a floured board. Cut out, using a special cutter if available, or a cardboard pattern and a sharp-pointed knife. Put the figures on to the baking tray and add currants to represent eyes and buttons. Bake for about 15 minutes and allow to cool before removing from the baking tray.

Working the dry ingredients into the creamed mixture, adding the syrup, shaping and decorating

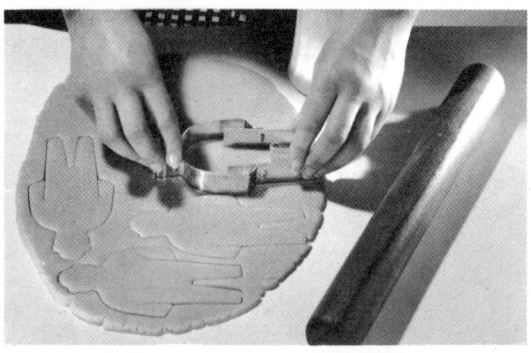

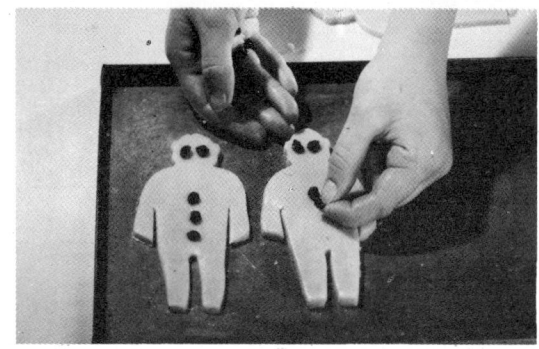

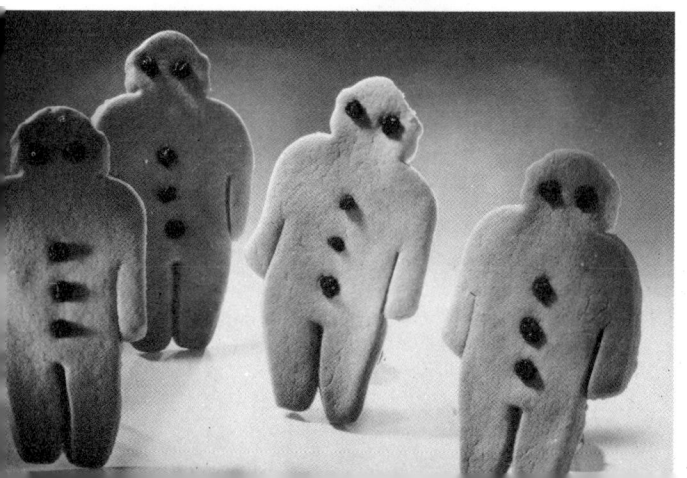

Cooking Equipment

Excellent meals can be produced with surprisingly little equipment, but it does make the work easier if you have the right utensils and a few labour-saving devices that you can really use.

Make your own list of the basic items, using the notes below as a guide but bearing in mind your own circumstances. As storage space and cash allow, you can then add other more expensive and specialised items which you would like. Avoid buying odd gadgets unless you are sure they will do a real job for you.

Choosing equipment can be tricky because of the wide variety on sale. However, Good Housekeeping Institute is constantly testing household goods and will be glad to advise you on buying an article which is suited to your purpose, well-designed, well-made and efficient.

Pots and Pans
3 saucepans with lids—
  2-pint, 3-pint, 8-pint
1½-pint milk saucepan, with non-stick finish, for sauces, etc.
8-inch frying pan of fairly heavy quality
4-pint kettle
Preserving pan
Pressure cooker (optional)

Kitchen China and Ovenware
Mixing bowl
2 pudding basins—1-pint and 1½-pint
1½-pint glass casserole with lid that can be used separately
4-pint casserole
2 plates
Jelly mould
Coffee pot or percolator

Baking Tins
Set of bun tins
7-inch cake tin
9-inch cake tin (for the Christmas cake)
2 7-inch sandwich tins, 1–1½ inches deep
Swiss roll tin
7-inch pie plate
Baking sheet
Cooling tray
Set of pastry cutters
Meat tin

General
Kitchen scales
Chopping board
Pastry board
Rolling pin
Pastry brush
Flour dredger
Grater with 2 or 3 sizes of hole
Rotary egg whisk
Lemon squeezer
6-inch round wire or nylon mesh sieve
Colander
Can opener (wall-type if possible)

Cutlery, Spoons, Tools
2 wooden spoons
2 forks
2 tablespoons
2 teaspoons
Perforated spoon for frying
Apple corer/potato peeler
4 knives—1 chopping, 1 vegetable, 1 bread and 1 carving
Carving fork
Pair kitchen scissors
Corkscrew/bottle opener

Storage Equipment, etc.
Vegetable rack
Storage jars and containers
Bread bin
Cake and biscuit tins
Preserving jars
Garbage bin

Care of Cooking Equipment

Cookers
1. Turn off the gas or the electric current while cleaning the cooker.
2. Wipe off any spilt food as soon as possible, while the stove is still warm.
3. Once a week wash the inside of the oven with hot water and soapless detergent; wash any removable parts of the hob, the oven racks and so on.
4. If a neglected cooker needs more drastic treatment, use one of the special proprietary products.

Refrigerators
1. Wipe up any spilt food at once.
2. De-frost every week, or as directed by the makers.
3. After de-frosting, wash the refrigerator with a little bicarbonate of soda dissolved in luke-warm water, then dry it. Wash the metal parts with plain water; don't use soap or abrasive powders.

Saucepans, Frying Pans
1. Follow any special directions given by the manufacturers, especially for non-stick pans.
2. In general, soak saucepans immediately after use and wash them in hot water, using a stiff brush or saucepan cleaner (except for non-stick pans).
3. Don't use abrasive powders or soda.
4. Aluminium can be cleaned with soapless detergent and a nylon pot scourer. Use very fine steel wool if necessary to burnish outside of pans.

Cake Tins, Cutters, Metal Moulds, etc.
1. Wash tins in the normal way. Don't use abrasive powders, which may damage the surface.
2. Dry all tinned articles carefully; place them upside-down in a warm oven or on a rack to dry them off and prevent rusting.

Kitchen Knives
1. Stainless steel knives require no special polishing; they are simply washed and well dried.
2. Ordinary steel knives (which have the advantage that they can generally be given a sharper edge) must be washed immediately after use and need frequent cleaning with a cork or cloth dipped in a paste cleanser or mild abrasive.
3. Store knives separately, in a case, rack or baize-lined drawer, to retain their cutting edge. You will get more satisfactory results if you use each knife only for its intended purpose.

Mincers, Shredders and so on
1. Wash and dry them thoroughly after use, putting them in a warm oven or on a rack.
2. Reassemble the several parts when dry, keeping any special attachments or pieces together.

Sensible Shopping

Whether you make a detailed budget of all your household expenditure or just spend what you have to and hope for the best, one thing is certain: food is going to account for a great big slice of the budget. Of course you will want to get the best possible value for your money and it does pay to wander around comparing quality and prices in the different types of shop in your neighbourhood. You can often take advantage of special reduced prices on branded goods (it can be an expensive experiment to buy unknown goods simply because they are cheap) and you can find out if one shop is better than another for, say, cheese or bacon or tea. If there is a local market it is often cheaper to buy fresh fruit and vegetables there, but it is up to you to see that what you buy is in good condition—a stallholder often does not feel the same responsibility to his customers as a shopkeeper.

It is a good idea to keep a store of tinned foods and dry goods in packets, so that you have something in hand for emergencies. Things like this can be bought fortnightly or monthly as you need them. Perishable foods like butter, bacon and so on are best bought twice a week; meat, fish, vegetables and salads as you need them. You can tell fresh fish by its plump, shining appearance and clean smell, while fresh vegetables and salads look perky and crisp, never yellowing, wilted or dejected. Keep perishable foods in the refrigerator or in a cool, airy larder. Some refrigerators have special compartments for butter, salads and so on, which give ideal storage conditions.

Choosing meat is a bit of a problem as the price varies so much according to the cut. The most tender and well-flavoured joints, which are of course also the most expensive, are for roasting, grilling or frying, while the cheaper, more sinewy cuts are best cooked very slowly and are excellent braised or stewed. Both kinds of meat have equal food value. Unwrap meat when you get it home, and put it either just under the ice box in the refrigerator or, if you have no refrigerator, in a cool, airy place, covered with clean muslin or a wire-mesh cover so that the air can circulate round it. Do not leave it standing in its own juice, or in a warm place, or it will go bad quickly. If you have to leave raw meat in the refrigerator for more than an hour or two, wrap it loosely in a polythene bag or a strip of polythene film, to keep it in good condition.

Family Catering

These are the approximate quantities to allow per head per meal.

Meat and Fish
Meat: with bone	4–6 oz.
boneless	4 oz.
Fish: with much bone	6–8 oz.
with little or no bone	4 oz.

Vegetables (weight as purchased)
Beans (broad)	$\frac{1}{2}$–$\frac{3}{4}$ lb.
Beans (runner)	6 oz.
Brussels Sprouts	6–8 oz.
Cabbage	6–8 oz.
Carrots	4–6 oz.
Celery	1 large head for 4 persons
Curly Kale	6–8 oz.
Greens (Spring)	6–8 oz.
Onions	6 oz.
Parsnips	6 oz.
Peas (green)	$\frac{1}{2}$ lb.
Peas (dried)	2 oz.
Potatoes	$\frac{1}{2}$ lb.
Seakale	4 oz.
Spinach	$\frac{1}{2}$–$\frac{3}{4}$ lb.
Swedes	$\frac{1}{2}$ lb.
Turnips	$\frac{1}{2}$ lb.

Cereals
Rice (for curry, etc.)	1–2 oz.
Macaroni	1–1$\frac{1}{2}$ oz.
Oatmeal (for porridge)	1–1$\frac{1}{2}$ oz.

Puddings
Sponge or suet puddings	1$\frac{1}{2}$ oz. flour, etc.
Pastry (for pies and puddings)	1$\frac{1}{2}$ oz. flour, etc.
Milk pudding, moulds, jellies	$\frac{1}{4}$ pt. milk
Junket	$\frac{1}{4}$ pt. milk
Fruit (pies, puddings)	4–5 oz. fruit
Custard (as a sauce)	$\frac{1}{8}$ pt. milk
Batter (Yorkshire Pudding)	1 oz. flour

Beverages
Coffee (breakfast)	1 tbsp.
Coffee (after-dinner)	1 dessertsp.
Tea	1 tsp.

Miscellaneous
Soup	$\frac{1}{4}$–$\frac{1}{3}$ pint
Sauces and gravies	$\frac{1}{8}$ pint

Foods in Season

January
Cod, haddock, herring.
Beetroot, broccoli, Brussels sprouts, cabbage, carrots, celery, chicory, leeks, lettuce, mushrooms, onions, potatoes, swedes, tomatoes, turnips.
Apples, bananas, grapes, grapefruit, lemons, oranges, pears, rhubarb (forced).

February
Cod, haddock, herring.
Beetroot, broccoli, Brussels sprouts, cabbage, carrots, celery, chicory, leeks, lettuce, mushrooms, onions, potatoes, swedes, tomatoes, turnips.
Apples, bananas, grapes, grapefruit, lemons, oranges, rhubarb (forced).

March
Cod, haddock, herring.
Beetroot, broccoli, Brussels sprouts, cabbage, carrots, cauliflower, celery, chicory, cress, cucumbers, leeks, lettuce, mushrooms, onions, potatoes, tomatoes, turnips.
Apples, bananas, grapefruit, lemons, oranges, rhubarb (forced).

April
Cod, haddock, herring, mackerel.
Beetroot, broccoli, cabbage, carrots, cauliflower, cress, cucumbers, leeks, lettuce, mushrooms, onions, potatoes, spinach, tomatoes, turnips.
Apples, apricots, bananas, grapes, grapefruit, lemons, oranges, rhubarb (forced).

May
Haddock, kipper, mackerel, plaice.
Beetroot, cabbage, carrots, cauliflower, cress, cucumbers, leeks, lettuce, mushrooms, onions, peas, potatoes, spinach, tomatoes, turnips.
Apples, apricots, bananas, grapes, grapefruit, lemons, oranges, rhubarb.

June
Haddock, kipper, mackerel, plaice.
Beetroot, broad beans, cabbage, carrots, cauliflower, cress, cucumbers, leeks, lettuce, mushrooms, onions, peas, potatoes, spinach, tomatoes, turnips.
Apples, apricots, bananas, cherries, gooseberries, grapes, grapefruit, lemons, oranges, raspberries, redcurrants, strawberries.

July
Haddock, kipper, mackerel, plaice.
Beetroot, broad beans, cabbage, carrots, cauliflower, cress, cucumbers, leeks, lettuce, marrows, mushrooms, onions, peas, potatoes, spinach, tomatoes, turnips.
Apples, apricots, bananas, cherries, gooseberries, grapefruit, lemons, oranges, plums, red-currants.

August
Haddock, kipper, mackerel, plaice.
Beetroot, broad beans, cabbage, carrots, cauliflower, cress, cucumbers, French beans, leeks, lettuce, marrows, mushrooms, onions, peas, potatoes, spinach, tomatoes, turnips.
Apples, apricots, bananas, grapes, grapefruit, lemons, oranges, peaches, plums.

September
Cod, haddock, herring, mackerel, plaice.
Beetroot, cabbage, carrots, cauliflower, celery, cress, cucumbers, French beans, leeks, lettuce, marrows, mushrooms, onions, potatoes, spinach, tomatoes, turnips.
Apples, bananas, blackberries, grapes, grapefruit, lemons, oranges, peaches, pears, plums.

October
Cod, haddock, herring, mackerel, plaice.
Beetroot, broccoli, Brussels sprouts, cabbage, carrots, cauliflower, celery, chicory, cucumbers, French beans, leeks, lettuce, mushrooms, onions, potatoes, swedes, tomatoes, turnips.
Apples, bananas, grapes, grapefruit, lemons, oranges, pears.

November
Cod, haddock, herring, plaice.
Beetroot, broccoli, Brussels sprouts, cabbage, carrots, cauliflower, celery, chicory, leeks, lettuce, mushrooms, onions, potatoes, swedes, tomatoes, turnips.
Apples, bananas, grapes, grapefruit, lemons, oranges, pears.

December
Cod, haddock, herring, plaice.
Beetroot, broccoli, Brussels sprouts, cabbage, carrots, celery, chicory, leeks, lettuce, mushrooms, onions, potatoes, swedes, tomatoes, turnips.
Apples, bananas, grapes, grapefruit, lemons, oranges, pears, rhubarb.

Glossary of Cooking Terms

Baking: The term used for cooking in an oven by dry heat. Most cakes and pastries and many puddings and savoury dishes are baked. Meat cooked in the oven, however, is usually referred to as roast.

Baking Blind: See page 96.

Basting: Pouring hot fat or liquid over food (particularly meat or poultry) at intervals during the cooking, to prevent it becoming dry on the outside.

Beating: Agitating an ingredient or a mixture by vigorously turning it over and over with an upward motion, in order to incorporate air; a spoon, fork, whisk or electric mixer may be used.

To beat raw meat is to hit it briskly all over the surface with a rolling pin or something similar so as to break down the fibres and make the meat more tender when cooked.

Blanching: Putting food in cold water and just bringing it to the boil. After this it is drained and usually put into cold water.

Almonds and chestnuts are blanched to remove the skin. White meats and vegetables are sometimes blanched in order to preserve their colour, while onions or other strong-tasting foods may be blanched to make their flavour blander.

Blending: Mixing flour, cornflour or similar ground grain with a cold liquid, such as water, milk or stock, to form a smooth paste. This is usually done before the hot liquid for a sauce, the thickening for a soup, stew and so on, is added and it prevents lumps forming. A spoon is the best implement for blending.

Boiling: Cooking in boiling liquid. This is the method generally used for cooking vegetables, rice and other cereals.

Bouquet Garni: A bunch of three or four herbs, selected from marjoram, thyme, parsley, bay leaf, used to add flavour to soups and stews. The herbs are usually tied in a piece of muslin and taken out before the dish is served, or when the flavour has become pronounced enough.

Braising: A combination of roasting, stewing and steaming, suitable for meat and rabbit, etc. Brown the food lightly in a little hot dripping, then place it on a bed of cut-up vegetables, such as carrots, onion and so on, with just enough liquid to cover the vegetables. Put on the lid and cook slowly in a slow oven or over a gentle heat.

Braising is also the term used to describe the cooking of vegetables such as carrots, celery and onions in a similar way.

Browning: Giving a dish (usually already cooked) an appetising golden-brown colour by placing it under the grill or in a hot oven for a short time.

To Casserole: Cooking meat, poultry, etc., slowly in the oven in a covered casserole dish.

Consistency: The term used to describe the texture of a cake or pudding mixture before it is cooked.

Pouring Consistency: The mixture should be soft enough to be poured steadily from a bowl to a tin and just find its own level.

Coating Consistency: The mixture should be thick enough to coat the back of a spoon.

Dropping Consistency: Fill a spoon with some of the mixture and hold it on its side over the bowl without jerking—the mixture should fall off after a few seconds.

Stiff Consistency: The mixture should just hold its own shape.

Creaming: Beating fat and sugar together with a wooden spoon until the mixture is light and creamy in both colour and texture. It is the process used for many cake and pudding mixtures. An electric mixer enables creaming to be done very quickly and efficiently.

Draining: The two main methods of removing surplus liquid or fat from foods are by means of a sieve or colander or by placing the food on crumpled absorbent kitchen paper.

Dredging: The action of sprinkling food lightly and evenly with flour, sugar, etc. Fish and meat are often dredged with flour before frying, while cakes, biscuits, pancakes, etc., may be sprinkled with fine sugar to improve their appearance. A dredger—a pierced container of metal or plastic—is usually used.

Egg and Crumbing: Food which is to be fried or baked is sometimes coated first with egg and breadcrumbs. Sift some fine fresh breadcrumbs (browned breadcrumbs are suitable only for coating already cooked food, such as ham) and put them on kitchen paper. Put some beaten egg (or egg mixed with an equal quantity of milk or water) on a plate. Toss the food in seasoned flour, then put it in the egg, brushing it all over with a pastry brush. Lift it with a wide-bladed knife, hold it for a moment to drain and lay it on the breadcrumbs. Holding opposite corners of the paper, toss the crumbs over the food, then lift it out and pass it from one hand to the other till all loose crumbs have fallen off.

Flouring: Dredging flour over the surface of a food in order to dry it or coat it for frying, or sprinkling flour over a pastry board before use.

Folding in: A method of combining whisked or creamed mixtures with other ingredients to retain lightness. It is usually done with a metal spoon, which is drawn across the bottom of the bowl, taking up a spoonful of the mixture and bringing it over the dry ingredients on top, thus "folding" them in. The process is repeated till the

Glossary of Cooking Terms (continued)

two mixtures are combined. It must be done very lightly—beating or violently agitating the mixture might cause some of the bubbles in it to be broken down.

Frying: Cooking food in hot fat by one of two methods:
1. In shallow-fat-frying the food is never more than a third covered by the fat and some foods—such as chops, fillets of fish and sausages—require only enough fat to prevent them from sticking to the pan. Made-up dishes such as hamburgers and fish cakes require rather more fat.

Cook the food on both sides to brown it lightly, then reduce the heat so that it cooks more gently. When it is done, lift it out of the pan and drain off excess fat. Put on to crumpled kitchen paper to finish draining.

2. For deep fat frying, the fat must be deep enough to cover the food. It may be used again and again, provided it is strained after use. All food fried in deep fat (except potatoes, pastry and doughnuts), should be coated in batter or egg and breadcrumbs.

The temperature of the fat may be tested as follows: If a 1-inch cube of crustless, stale white bread browns in 60–70 seconds, the fat is hot enough for uncooked foods, such as apple fritters. If the bread browns in 40–50 seconds, the fat is hot enough for cooked foods such as fish cakes. If the bread browns in 20–30 seconds, the fat is hot enough for wet cold foods, such as fish in batter.

Alternatively, drop in a piece of raw potato. If there is slight bubbling round the potato after a few seconds, the temperature is too low for most cooking. If there is moderate bubbling after a few seconds, the food can be put into the fat, but the heat must be maintained so that the temperature of the fat is not lowered by the addition of the cold food. If there is fast bubbling the fat is too hot and the heat should be reduced before the food is put in. (This potato test is not so accurate as the first one, using bread.)

Lower the food gently into the fat, using a basket. (Draw the pan away from the heat while doing this and return it immediately the food is submerged.) Cook until golden-brown and drain thoroughly before serving.

Glazing: Giving food a glossy surface. Pastry, scones and yeast mixtures can be brushed before baking with beaten egg or milk, or a sweet glaze made by dissolving 2 level tbsps. of sugar in 1 tbsp. water. New carrots, potatoes, etc., are tossed in butter or margarine to glaze them and meat, poultry and fish can be glazed with aspic jelly.

Grilling: Cooking food in direct heat under a griller.

Poaching: Cooking gently in liquid which is just below boiling point. (See poached Eggs and Poached Fish.)

To Purée: Passing vegetables or fruit (usually cooked) through a sieve, to remove skins, fibres and pips and give a smooth, even texture.

Roasting: Generally taken to mean cooking meat and poultry in hot fat in the oven. Potatoes and parsnips, etc., may also be cooked by this method. Meat and poultry are also sometimes roasted on a revolving spit.

Roux: A mixture of equal quantities of fat and flour cooked together for a few minutes. The mixture is frequently used as foundation for sauces.

Rubbing in: A method of mixing fat and flour used in making plain cakes, shortcrust pastry, etc. First cut the fat into small pieces in the flour, then rub the fat into the flour with the fingertips, lifting the mixture well out of the bowl to incorporate air at the same time.

To Sauté: Cooking food in fat without browning it. The ingredients (usually vegetables) are shaken or tossed in the hot fat in a saucepan with a lid on. This improves their flavour without colouring the soup or other dish in which they are used. For Sauté Potatoes, see page 60.

Separating Eggs: Dividing the white from the yolk (as when making meringue). Crack the egg sharply and open the crack only just enough to let the white slip out into a cup; tip the yolk carefully from one half of the shell to the other to release all the white.

Sieving: Rubbing or pressing food (e.g., cooked vegetables) through a sieve; a wooden spoon is used to force it through: see Purée.

Sifting: Shaking flour and similar dry ingredients through a sieve. If more than one ingredient is being used, they should be mixed before sifting.

Simmering: Keeping a cooking liquid at just below boiling point. Bring to the boil, then adjust the heat so that the surface of the liquid just moves but does not bubble.

Steaming: Cooking food in the steam from boiling water, preferably in a steamer with perforated base placed over an ordinary saucepan. Small pieces of food requiring only short steaming time may be cooked on a covered greased plate over a pan of boiling water. Steaming takes about half as long again as boiling and the water must be kept on the boil, being replenished from time to time with boiling water from a kettle.

Stewing: Cooking slowly just below boiling point in a covered container, with just enough liquid to cover the food—usually meat, poultry, game or fruit.

Whisking or Whipping: Beating up cream, jelly, eggs or liquids rapidly, to incorporate air or to give a pleasing fluffy texture. It may be done with a fork, wire whisk, rotary whisk or electric mixer, and is usually continued until the food is quite stiff.

The term whisking is also used for the combining of eggs and sugar for sponge cake mixtures.

Cooking Guide

Working from a Recipe

1. Before you start to make a dish, read the recipe right through and read also any general instructions at the beginning of the section or chapter.

2. Next, collect together the cooking utensils you will need and do any preliminary preparation, such as greasing dishes, lining cake tins and so on. If the dish is to be baked, turn on the heat and set the thermostatic control so that the oven will be at the correct temperature when you are ready for it.

3. Finally, collect and measure out all the ingredients needed. If you are a beginner, it is sensible to follow the recipe exactly, scrupulously weighing and measuring the ingredients—leave variations for when you have more experience. Amounts of flavourings, seasonings and spices, sweetening, etc., may usually be varied to suit individual tastes, but basic ingredients like flour or fat should not be altered.

4. Follow closely the directions given in the recipe—seemingly slight changes in procedure may make all the difference between an outstanding dish and one that is only mediocre.

5. For the most part, unless otherwise stated, the amounts given in these recipes are sufficient for 4 people. For smaller dishes you will generally find it quite simple to halve the ingredients. Do not, however, just halve the cooking time: the meat in a stew takes the same length of time to cook, even though there is only half as much of it, while for a baked dish the cooking time will need to be reduced only by about a quarter when the recipe is halved. For boiled or steamed meat or fish, on the other hand, the cooking time depends on the size of the piece to be cooked.

Generally speaking, it is not really safe to make more than a double quantity of any recipe, as after that, proportions may vary. If you need a larger amount, it is better to make several batches.

Oven Temperatures

In this book the method of quoting oven temperatures reads thus: Fairly hot oven (400°F., mark 6). The degrees Fahrenheit give the temperature of the oven, and also the corresponding electric setting, while the phrase "mark 6" applies to the standard thermostatic setting of a modern gas cooker. The following table shows the range of temperatures:

Oven Description	Approx. F. temp., also electric setting	Standard gas thermostat
Very cool	250°	mark ¼
	275°	mark ½
Cool	300°	mark 1–2
Warm	325°	mark 3
Moderate	350°	mark 4
Fairly hot	375°	mark 5
	400°	mark 6
Hot	425°	mark 7
Very hot	450°	mark 8
	475°	mark 9

Note: These gas settings apply only to modern cookers; if you have an old model and are in doubt about the settings, ask your local Gas Board.

Oven Management

1. Arrange the oven shelves before the oven is heated.

2. Set the thermostat to the required temperature 15–20 minutes before the food is to be put in. (Some dishes, such as milk puddings and casseroles, which require very long, slow cooking, can "start from cold".)

3. The centre of the oven corresponds most exactly to the dial setting; the upper part is somewhat hotter, while the bottom of the oven is cooler.

4. Open the oven door as little as possible during the cooking time. With cakes in particular be very gentle, as an inrush of cold air may spoil the baking.

5. When using the oven for browning au gratin dishes, etc., have it very hot and place the dishes at the top, otherwise the mixture will bubble without browning.

6. Put pie dishes, casseroles, cake tins, etc., on baking sheets so that they are easier to move.

Weighing and Measuring

Weighing is the most reliable method of measuring for all but the smallest amounts. Quantities are therefore given in pounds and ounces, whenever possible.

When very small quantities are involved, however, or when kitchen scales are not available, ingredients must

Cooking Guide (continued)

be measured—usually in spoonfuls. In accordance with modern practice, we quote all quantities in terms of *level* spoonfuls, unless otherwise stated.

Since sizes of spoons vary, it is not possible to give exact equivalents in ounces, but the following is an approximate guide:

Flour, Cornflour, Cocoa, Custard Powder
1 oz. equals approximately 3 level tablespoonfuls.

Dried Fruit
1 oz. equals approximately 2 level tablespoonfuls.

Sugar, Rice, Lentils, etc.
1 oz. equals approximately 2 level tablespoonfuls.

Breadcrumbs (fresh)
¼ oz. equals approximately 1½ level tablespoonfuls.

Breadcrumbs (dry)
¼ oz. equals approximately 1 level tablespoonful.

Liquids
Whenever possible the amount of liquid required is specified in the recipes, but since some flours absorb more moisture than others, and eggs vary in size, the cook has to judge by experience the exact amount of liquid needed to obtain the correct consistency.

A graduated measure is of course the best means of measuring liquids, but as a very rough guide it can be taken that:
  1 teacup contains ⅓ pint
  1 tumbler or breakfast cup contains ½ pint
  8 tablespoonfuls equal ¼ pint.

Syrup and Treacle
The most practical method of measuring syrup is to use a warmed spoon; this enables a level tablespoonful to be taken from the tin without any extra syrup clinging to the underside of the spoon. Incidentally, 1 tbsp. of syrup weighs approximately 1½ oz.

Conversions

Mass
1 oz = 28·35 g
2 oz = 56·7 g
4 oz = 113·4 g
8 oz = 226·8 g
12 oz = 340·2 g
16 oz = 453·6 g
1 kilogramme = 2·2 lb

Abbreviations
oz = ounce(s)
ml = millimetre(s)
cm = centimetre(s)
g = gramme(s)

Temperature
32° F. = 0° Celsius
212°F. = 100°C.
225°F. = 107°C.
250°F. = 121°C.
275°F. = 135°C.
300°F. = 149°C.
325°F. = 163°C.
350°F. = 177°C.
375°F. = 190°C.
400°F. = 204°C.
425°F. = 218°C.
450°F. = 232°C.

Capacity
¼ pint = 142 ml
½ pint = 284 ml
1 pint = 568 ml
½ litre = 0·88 pint
1 litre = 1·76 pints

Length
1 inch = 2·54 cm
6 inches = 15·2 cm
100 cm = 1 metre
       = 39·37 inches

Note: To convert the recipes in this book to metric we have found that it is more practical to use the 25 g unit in place of the oz, the 5-ml spoon in place of the Teaspoon, the 15-ml spoon in place of the Tablespoon and to measure 500 ml to the Pint. Recipes converted in this manner will yield slightly less than the original so it is best to allow for slightly more meat, i.e. 450 g to the lb, where recipes containing meat are concerned, to ensure that they are nutritionally balanced.

The above is based on information agreed by the UK Federation for Education in Home Economics 1970.

Index

A Almond Fingers, 140
Paste, 152–153
Amber, Apricot, 98
Anchovy Sauce, 87
Apple(s) and Prune Stuffing, 90
Baked Stuffed, 107
Cake, 145
Charlotte, 118
Cornflake Crunch, 123
Fritters, 105
Muesli, 9
Pie, 93
Rings, 43
Stewed, 119
Apricot Amber, 98
Fool, 120

B Bacon, 12, 41
Omelette, 17
Roly-poly, 54
Stuffing, 90
Baked Apples, 107
Bacon, Gammon, 41
Chicken Joints, 59
Egg Custard Tart, 109
Eggs, 14
Fruit Batter, 106
Mushrooms, 63
Plaice with Mushrooms, 25
Potatoes (Jacket), 60
Salmon, 27
Stuffed Apples, 107
Stuffed Fish, 26
Stuffed Liver, 51
Tomatoes, 65
Baking, 167
Blind, 96
Tins, 164
Banana Split, 127
Basting, 33, 167
Batter(s), 102–106
Baked Fruit, 106
for Fish, 28
Beans, Broad, French, Runner, 65
Beating, 167
Beef, 38
Carving, 34, 35
Curried, 56
Roast, 33
Stew, 44
Beetroot, 64, 66
Belly of Pork, 40
Best End of Lamb, 34
Birthday Cake, 147 (Rich Fruit Cake), 153
Biscuits, 160–163
Black Coffee, 18
Blade of Pork, 40
Blanching, 167

Blancmange, Layered, 130
Blended Sauce, 88
Blending, 167
Boiled Bacon, Gammon, 41
Eggs, 14
Meat, 33
Potatoes, 60
Rice, 80
Spaghetti, 80
Vegetables, 62–65
Boiling, 167
Bolognese Spaghetti, 83
Bouquet Garni, 167
Braised Celery Hearts, 65
Braising, 167
Brandy Butter, 132
Bread, 134
Fried, 11
Sauce, 88
Breakfast, 8–19
Breast of Lamb, 34, 39
of Veal, 34
Brisket of Beef, 38
Broad Beans, 65
Brown Gravy, 88
Stew (Beef), 44
Browning, 167
Brussels Sprouts, 62
Buns, Rock, 137
Jam, 138
Butter, Brandy, 132
Cream, 154–155, 158–159

C Cabbage, 62, 66
Cake(s), 137–163
Apple, 145
Cherry, 146
Christmas, 150–153
Decorating, 152–159
Fairy, 158
Fruit, 144, 147
Ginger Loaf, 146
Icings, 152–157
Plain Fruit, 144
Queen, 139
Rich Fruit, 147
Sandwich, 148
Tins, 142, 164
Victoria Sandwich, 148
Walnut, 147
Walnut Loaf, 143
Caper Sauce, 87
Carrots, 64, 66
Carving Meat, 34–37
Casserole Cooking, 167
Liver, 50
Catering Quantities, 165

Index (continued)

Cauliflower, 62
Celery, 65, 66
  Soup, 85
  Stuffing, 90
Cereals, 10
Charlotte, Apple, 118
Cheese and Cheese Cookery, 72–79
  and Onion Pie, 77
  and Peach Salad, 69
  and Vegetable Flan, 75
  Course, 72
  Grated, 86
  Macaroni, 74
  Omelette, 17
  on Toast, 73
  Pudding, 76
  Sauce, 87
Cheesy Grilled Fish, 24
Cherry Cake, 146
Chicken, 58–59
  Soup, 86
Chipped Potatoes, 60
Chocolate Butter Cream, 154
  Fairy Cakes, 158
  Glacé Icing, 156
  Sandwich Cake, 148
  Sauce for Ice Cream, 132
Chops, Lamb, 39
  Pork, 40, 43
Christmas Cake, 150–153
  Puddings, 114, 115
Chuck Steak, 38
Coating Batter, 102
  Consistency, 167
Cobbler, Fruit, 117
Cocktail, Shellfish, 31
Coconut Tarts, 141
Cod, 20
Coffee, 18–19
  Butter Cream, 154
  Fairy Cakes, 158
  Glacé Icing, 156
  Sandwich Cake, 148
Cold Puddings, 120–130
Cole Slaw, 69
Condé, Peach, 125
Consistency, 167
Continental Cheeses, 72
Cookers, 164
Cooking Equipment, 164
  Guide, 169–170
  Terms, 167–168
Corn on the Cob, 65
Corned Beef Fritters, 105
Cornflake Crunch, Apple, 123
  Flan, Lemon, 129
Crackling, 33
Cream, 158
  Butter, 154–155, 158–159
  Cheese and Peach Salad, 69
  Sour, 86

Creamed Potatoes, 60
Creaming, 167
Cress, 66
Croûtons, 86
Crumb Crusts for Flans, 96
Crumble, Rhubarb, 116
Crunch, Apple Cornflake, 123
Cucumber, 66
Curried Beef, 56
  Mince, 57
Curry Sauce, 88
Custard Sauce, 131
  Tart, 109
  Tartlets, 94
Cutlery, Kitchen, 164
Cutlets, Lamb, 39
  Pork, 40

D Deep Fat Frying, 168
Draining, 167
Dredging, 167
Dressings, Salad, 68
Dried Fish, 13, 20
  Fruit, 9
Drop Scones, 136
Dropping Consistency, 167
Duck Eggs, 14

E Economical Christmas Pudding, 114
Egg(s), 14–17, 66, 168
  and Crumbing, 167
  Custard Tart, 109
  Custard Tartlets, 94
  Salad, 70
  Sauce, 87
English Cheeses, 72
Equipment, Cooking, 164

F Fairy Cakes, 158
Fillet(s), Fish, 13, 22
  of Beef, 34
  of Pork, 40
  of Veal, 34
Finnan Haddock, 20
Fish, 13, 20–32, 165
  Baked Stuffed, 26
  Cheesy Grilled, 24
  Fillets, Fried, 22
  in Batter, 28
  Omelette, 17
  Pie, 32
  Smoked, 13
Flan(s), 96–97
  Cheese and Vegetable, 75
  Lemon Cornflake, 129
  Pastry, 96
Flapjacks, Syrup, 162
Flouring, 167
Folding in, 167
Foods in Season, 166
Fool, Apricot, 120

Forcemeat Stuffing, 90
French Beans, 65
  Onion Soup, 84
  Salad Dressing, 68
Fricassee, Scallop, 30
Fried Bacon, 12
  Bread, 11
  Eggs, 14
  Fish Fillets, 22
  Fish in Batter, 28
  Herrings, 23
  Kidneys, 11
  Potatoes, 60
  Sausages, 11
Fritters, Apple, 105
  Savoury, 105
Fruit Batter, Baked, 106
  Cake, Plain, 144
  Cake, Rich, 147
  Cobbler, 117
  Dried, 9
  Flan, 96
  for Breakfast, 8–9
  in Jelly, 120
  Juice, 8
  Lattice Pie, 99
  Layer Pudding, 111
  Muesli, 9
  Pudding, Steamed, 112
  Salad, 124
  Trifle, 122
Frying, 168

G
Gammon, 41
Garnishes for Salads, 66–67
  for Soup, 86
Ginger Loaf Cake, 146
Gingerbread, 149
  Men, 163
Girdle Scones, 136
Glacé Icing, 156–159
Glaze for Baked Bacon, 41
  for Flans, 96
Glazing, 168
Golden Fillets, 13, 20
Goose Eggs, 14
Grapefruit, 8
Grated Cheese, 86
Gravy, 88
Green Peas, 64
  Peppers, Stuffed, 81
  Vegetables, 62
Greens, 62
Grilled Bacon, 12
  Fish, Cheesy, 24
  Kidneys, 11
  Mackerel, 23
  Mushrooms, 63
  Pork Chops, 43
  Salmon, 27

Grilled Sausages, 11
  Steak, 42
  Tomatoes, 11, 65
Grilling, 168

H
Haddock, 20
  Kedgeree, 29
  Smoked, 13, 20
Hake, 20
Halibut, 20
Ham and Leeks au Gratin, 79
  Omelette, 17
  Stuffing, 90
Herbs in Salads, 66
Herrings, 20
  Fried, 23
Hot Puddings, 105–119
Hot-pot, Lancashire, 48

I
Ice Cream, 126
  Cream, Sauce for, 132
Iced Cakes, 150–159
Icing, Almond, 152
  Butter, 154
  Glacé, 156
  Royal, 153
Individual Custard Tarts, 94
Irish Stew, 45

J
Jacket Potatoes, 60
Jam Buns, 138
  Roly-Poly, 110
  Sauce, 131
  Sponge, Steamed, 113
  Tarts, 94
Jammy Rings, 161
Jelly Sweets, 120–121
  Whip, 120

K
Kedgeree, 29
Kidney(s), 11
  Omelette, 17
  Soup, 86
Kippers, 13, 20
Kitchen Equipment, 164,
Knives, 34, 164

L
Lamb, 39
  Carving, 34, 36
  Roast, 33
Lancashire Hot-pot, 48
Lattice Pie, Fruit, 99
Layer Pudding, Fruit, 111
  Pudding, Syrup, 111
Layered Blancmange, 130
Leeks, 63
  and Ham au Gratin, 79
Leg of Beef, 38
  of Lamb, 36, 39
  of Pork, 34

Index (continued)

Lemon Butter Cream, 154
  Cornflake Flan, 129
  Fairy Cakes, 158
  Glacé Icing, 156
  Sandwich Cake, 148
  Sauce, 131
Lentil Soup, 85
Lettuce, 66
Lining Cake Tins, 142
Liquids, 170
Liver Casserole, 50
  Baked Stuffed, 51
Loaf Cakes, 143, 146
  Meat, 49
  Quick Wholemeal, 134
Loin of Lamb, 39
  of Pork, 37, 40

M

Macaroni Cheese, 74
Mackerel, 20
  Grilled, 23
Marmalade Sauce, 132
Marrow, 63
Mashed Potatoes, 60
Measuring, 169–170
Meat, 33–57, 165
  Boiled, 33
  Fritters, 105
  Loaf, 49
  Pasties, 53
  Pie, 52
  Roast, 33
Middle End of Lamb, 39
Milk Puddings, 108–109
Mince, Curried, 57
  Pies, 100
Mint, 66
  Sauce, 88
Mixed Vegetable Soup, 84
Mocha Butter Cream, 154
  Fairy Cakes, 158
Muesli, Swiss Apple, 9
Mushroom(s), 63
  Omelette, 17
  Sauce, 87
  Stuffing, 90
Mustard and Cress, 66
Mutton: see Lamb

N

Noodles, 80
  with Tomato Sauce, 82

O

Omelette, Oven, 78
  Tomato, 17
  Variations, 17
Onion(s), 63
  and Cheese Pie, 77
  Sauce, 87
  Soup, French, 84
  Spring, 66

Orange(s), 8
  Butter Cream, 154
  Fairy Cakes, 158
  Glacé Icing, 156
  Salad, 70
  Sandwich Cake, 148
  Sauce, 131
Oven Management, 169
  Omelette, 78
  Temperatures, 169
Ovenware, 164

P

Pancakes, 103
  Scotch, 136
Parsley, 66
  Sauce, 87
Parsnips, 64
Pasta, 80, 82–83
Pasties, Meat, 53
Pastry, 92–101
  Flan, 96
  Shortcrust, 92
  Suetcrust: see Jam Roly-Poly, 110
Peach and Cream Cheese Salad, 69
  Condé, 125
Pear Sundae, 127
Peas, Green, 64
Peppers, Green, 81
Pie, Cheese and Onion, 77
  Fish, 32
  Fruit Lattice, 99
  Mince, 100
  Plate Apple, 93
  Steak and Mushroom, 52
Plaice, 20
  Baked, 25
Plain Fruit Cake, 144
Plate Apple Pie, 93
Poached Eggs, 14
  Haddock, 13
Poaching, 168
Popovers, 104
Pork, 40
  Carving, 34, 37
  Chops, Grilled, 43
  Roast, 33
Porridge, 10
Potato(es), 60–61
  Salad, 70
  Soup, 84
Pots and Pans, 164
Poultry, 58–59
Pouring Consistency, 167
Prune and Apple Stuffing, 90
Pudding(s), Cheese, 76
  Christmas, 114, 115
  Cold, 120–130
  Fruit, 112
  Fruit Layer, 111
  Hot, 105, 106, 107–119

Pudding(s), Milk, 108-109
  Rice, 108
  Semolina, 108
  Steak and Kidney, 55
  Steamed, 110-115
  Syrup Layer, 111
  Yorkshire, 104
Purée, 168

Q

Quantities, Catering, 165
Queen Cakes, 139
Quick Iced Cakes, 158
  Rolls, 133
  Wholemeal Loaves, 134

R

Radishes, 66
Recipes, to Use, 169
Refrigerators, 164
Rhubarb Crumble, 116
Rib of Beef, 35, 38
Rice, 80-81
  Pudding, 108
Rich Chocolate Sauce for
  Ice Cream, 132
  Christmas Pudding, 114
  Fruit Cake, 147
  Lemon or Orange Sauce, 131
Roast Chicken, 58
  Meat, 33
  Potatoes, 60
Roasting, 168
Rock Buns, 137
Rolled Oats, 10
Rolls, Quick, 133
Roly-Poly, Bacon, 54
  Jam, 110
Root Vegetables, 64
Rosy Fish Pie, 32
Roux, 168
  Sauce, White, 87
Royal Icing, 153
Rubbing in, 168
Runner Beans, 65

S

Saddle of Lamb, 34
Sage and Onion Stuffing, 90
Salad(s), 66-71
  Cream, 51, 68
  Dressings, 68
  Fruit, 124
Salmon, 20
  Baked, 27
  Grilled, 27
Salt Meat, 33
Sandwich Cake, Victoria, 148
Saucepans, 164
Sauce(s), 87-89, 131-132
  Meat, for Pasta, 83
  Savoury, 87-89
  Sweet, 131-132

Sauce, Tomato, for Pasta, 82
Sausage(s), 11
  Garnish for Soup, 86
  Rolls, 101
  Stuffing, 90
Sauté, 168
  Mushrooms, 63
  Potatoes, 60
Savoury Fritters, 105
  Sauces, 87-89
Scallop(s), 30
  Fricassee, 30
Scones, 135-136
  Drop, 136
Scotch Pancakes, 136
Scrag End of Lamb, 39
Scrambled Eggs, 14
Seasonable Foods, 166
Semolina Pudding, 108
Separating Eggs, 168
Shallow Frying, 168
Shellfish Cocktail, 31
Shin of Beef, 38
Shopping, 165
Shortbread, 160
Shortcake, Strawberry, 128
Shortcrust Pastry, 92
Shoulder of Lamb, 36, 39
  Steak, 38
Shrimp Sauce, 87
Sieving, 168
Sifting, 168
Simmering, 168
Sirloin of Beef, 35, 38
Slaw, Cole, 69
Small Cakes, Iced, 158-159
Smoked Fish, 13, 20
Soft Fruit Juice, 8
Sole, 20
Soup(s), 84-86
  Garnishes, 86
Sour Cream Garnish for
  Soup, 86
Spaghetti, Boiled, 80
  Bolognese, 83
Spare Rib of Pork, 34, 40
Spinach, 62
Sponge, Steamed Jam, 113
Spoons, Kitchen, 164
Spring Greens, 62
  Onions, 66
Sprouts, 62
Steak and Kidney Pudding, 55
  and Mushroom Pie, 52
  Grilled, 42
  Stewing, 38
Steamed Fruit Pudding, 112
  Jam Sponge, 113
  Meat Pudding, 55
  Puddings, 110-115
Steaming, 168

Index (continued)

Stew, Beef, 44
  Irish, 45
  Summer, 47
  Veal, 46
Stewed Apples, 119
Stewing, 168
Stiff Consistency, 167
Stock for Soups, 86
Storage Equipment, 164
Strawberry Shortcake, 128
Stuffed Baked Apples, 107
  Baked Fish, 26
  Breast of Lamb or Veal, 34
  Green Peppers, 81
  Liver, Baked, 51
Stuffings, 40, 90–91
Suetcrust pastry: see Jam
  Roly-Poly, 110
Summer Stew, 47
Sundae, Pear, 127
Swedes, 64
Sweet Corn, 65
  Sauces, 131–132
Swiss Apple Muesli, 9
Syrup Flapjacks, 162
  Layer Pudding, 111
  Sauce, 132
  Tart, 95

T Tart(s), Baked Egg Custard, 109
  Coconut, 141
  Individual Custard, 94
  Jam, 94
  Syrup, 95
Temperatures, Oven, 169
Tins, Baking, 164
  Cake, 142, 164
Toad in the Hole, 106
Toasted Croûtons, 86

Tomato(es), 65, 66
  Grilled, 11
  Omelette, 17
  Salad, 70
  Sauce for Pasta, 82
  Soup, 85
Tools, Kitchen, 164
Topside of Beef, 38
Treacle, to Measure, 170
Trifle, Fruit, 122
Turbot, 20
Turkey Eggs, 14
Turnips, 64

V Veal, Carving, 34
  Roast, 33
  Stew, 46
Vegetable(s), 60–65
  and Cheese Flan, 75
  Marrow, 63
  Soup, 84
Victoria Sandwich Cake, 148

W Walnut Butter Cream, 154
  Cake, 147
  Loaf Cake, 143
Watercress, 66
Weighing, 169
Whip, Jelly, 120
Whipping, 168
Whisking, 168
White Blended Sauce, 88
  Roux Sauce, 87
  Sauce, Sweet, 131
Wholemeal Loaves, Quick, 134
Winter Salads, 70

Y Yorkshire Pudding, 104